The
Information
Society

The Information Society

A Retrospective View

Herbert S. Dordick
Georgette Wang

SAGE Publications
International Educational and Professional Publisher
Newbury Park   London   New Delhi

For information address:

SAGE Publications, Inc.
2455 Teller Road
Newbury Park, California 91320

SAGE Publications Ltd.
6 Bonhill Street
London EC2A 4PU
United Kingdom

SAGE Publications India Pvt. Ltd.
M-32 Market
Greater Kailash I
New Delhi 110 048 India

Printed in the United States of America

Library of Congress Cataloging-in-Publication Data

Dordick, Herbert S., 1925-
   The information society: a retrospective view / Herbert S. Dordick,
Georgette Wang.
      p.   cm.
   Includes bibliographical references and index.
   ISBN 0-8039-4186-2. — ISBN 0-8039-4187-0 (pbk.)
   1. Information technology.   2. Economic development.
3. Information society.   I. Wang, Georgette.   II. Title.
HC79.I55D67   1993
303.48′3—dc20   93-3654
                                                                CIP

              95   96   10   9   8   7   6   5   4   3   2

Sage Production Editor: Judith L. Hunter

Contents

Preface

Have modern information technology and telecommunications heralded a new society, and a new man and woman? Has the Industrial Revolution been replaced by the information revolution, with none of the disbenefits of the former? This book examines to what extent an information society has emerged, and whether the promises of the past 30 or more years have been met. Recognizing that the enthusiasm for radical change in the highly industrialized world has spilled over into the newly industrialized nations and, indeed, to the yet-to-be-industrialized world, this book explores the consequences for these nations as well.

Looking for the information society is made more difficult by the enormous amount of data, scattered widely among numerous sources not easily amenable to either longitudinal analysis within a country or comparative analysis among countries. Without some limiting definitions of just what we mean by an information society and how to look for that society, nothing more than another historical overview would emerge. That is not to say that this would not be of value, especially if given a fresh interpretation. However, we have sought to do more. We have taken two preliminary steps before embarking on this search. First, we have defined *informatization* along three primary dimensions: infrastructure, economic, and social, and we have selected what we believe to be key measures for defining each of these dimensions. Second, we have selected 19 countries, which we have categorized as high-, middle-, and low-income nations by Gross Domestic Product per capita, on which to focus our analyses. We limit our data search within these boundaries.

Defining an information society is a difficult task; however, what can be described, if not entirely defined, is economic development or growth. We suggest that the economic growth or development process requires the integration of technology, social change, and economic change. We try to understand and present to the reader how the dimensions of our analysis and the measures chosen contribute to informatization and to economic growth.

We do not propose to perform rigid statistical analyses, seeking correlations between our measures and GNP/capita. The data with which we have worked does not permit this sophistication. Rather, we wish to determine whether there is sufficient evidence, based upon our limited analyses, to suppose that there are meaningful relationships between these measures and economic growth. Sufficient, to our way of thinking, means satisfying the needs of national planners to gain some insight into the consequences of the decisions they need to make.

This is an unusually appropriate time to revisit the claims that have been made for the emerging information society. Personal computers have been available in almost every industrialized country and in many newly emerging nations. Many pilot informatization schemes, aimed at business and the home, in Japan, Singapore, France and West Germany have been accomplished, and in France information services have been marketed for more than 5 years. In the United States network information services have been available for more than 15 years. Business and industry are utilizing network information services and are creating a marketplace on many networks. Educators, scientists, and engineers trained during this era have entered schools and universities. They are training graduates that will further expand the utilization of information technology and, thereby, lead to the development of an informatized nation.

Finding answers to these questions is critical to economic planners of all nations, from the most highly developed to those still seeking to enter into the global economy by becoming information societies. Almost all nations have chosen informatization as the most promising means for achieving this goal. Those few of the least-developed nations, in Africa, for example, are very likely to do so after they have achieved some measure of political stability. Indeed, many see economic growth as a means for achieving political stability. They will also choose informatization as the means by which to achieve this goal.

Acknowledgments

We wish to thank Darryl Chiu, Shuli Chen, and Yuan Jun for their assistance in gathering data from the wide variety of sources they had to comb and for performing the computer analyses from which we have drawn our conclusions.

We also wish to thank our families for showing infinite patience with us during the writing of this book.

1

Introduction

In 1963 Tadeo Umesao, a professor at Kyoto University in Japan, forecast the coming of an information industry; that was 30 years ago. In the late 1960s Daniel Bell, a Harvard professor, proposed the idea of a knowledge-based postindustrial society. This was more than 25 years ago. In the late 1970s Dordick and his colleagues at the University of Southern California suggested that with modern telecommunications and information technology, the industrialized nations were creating a marketplace on a network, a marketplace in which information goods and services would be bought and sold as if in a goods marketplace. And in 1981 Frederick Williams proclaimed the arrival of a communication revolution.

Over the past three decades we have witnessed both the worldwide growth of an information industry and the definition of a new economic

AUTHORS' NOTE: The data for this Introduction were drawn from a wide variety of sources, including recent newspapers and magazine articles, trade journals, scholarly articles, and government reports, including those of the United Nations, World Bank, and European Economic Community. Many of these sources will be referenced in subsequent chapters.

1

sector, the information sector. Repeatedly we are told that the industrial age is declining and in its place will be the information age. And in this new age our lives will be cleaner, greener, more pleasant, more intellectual, perhaps even less manic because we shall value ideas rather than things. In the cusp of this new era, are we better off today than we were before? Is this the information society?

In a sense, we are getting used to a way of life that has all of the earmarks of an information age as described by Umesao, Bell, Dordick, and Williams. At a critical moment just before the Gulf war became hot, President Bush showed the world how it was possible to stay in command while playing golf, the modern commander-in-chief commanding from his golf cart. While "telecommanding" may be new, "telebanking" is a reality, with banks now offering this service by computer-to-computer communications and by telephone. Many individuals are "teleshopping" by telephone and fax, and others are using personal computers to place their orders and arrange their travel plans. Education-at-a-distance, or "telelearning" using television has been initiated in Colombia, in India, by the Open University in the United Kingdom, and the University of Mid-America in Nebraska. Recently the computer and facsimile have joined in these classrooms without walls. From Bangkok and London to New York, people are walking, eating, riding subways and railroads, or enjoying the ocean sun and breezes on the beach with their radios, cellular fax-phones, and laptop computers at their sides. We ask for information by telephone and a voice synthesizer responds—science fiction only a few years ago, but today we are not surprised. The explosive diffusion of computers, telecommunications, broadcast and video media, and the information media is seen in national and global statistics. Almost half of the workers in the industrialized world are employed by the rapidly growing information industries, and in almost every industry there are workers whose primary tasks are to create, collect, process, and distribute information. The value added of information products and services to the United States Gross National Product is, today, slightly greater than 45%, and for Europe and Japan somewhat more than 40%. The world information industry, even if narrowly defined (and we shall be examining this definition), will be greater than $500 billion before the end of the decade. The production, processing, and distribution of information is a major industry throughout the world. By the year 2000, it will account for about 40% of the world's industrial production.

The global market for computer products scored an 8.9% growth to $278.5 billion in 1990, which was up from the 5.3% growth in the previous year. IBM's revenue rose to $67 billion during 1990, equivalent to Israel's and Singapore's combined Gross Domestic Product—and this in a recession year. Growth in information services has kept pace with computer industry growth most impressively; the U.S. Department of Commerce reported a 20% growth in on-line information services. With 4,500 databases available worldwide, the database market is estimated to be in the neighborhood of $6-$7 billion. The market continues to grow rapidly.

Notebook computers exceed the computing power of yesterday's room-size computers, and smart shoppers can purchase them for a fraction of the cost of the early business computers. In the next several years, certainly before the year 2000, the sales of these portable computers, which accompany the information worker to the beach and to the board meeting, will more than triple. The power of today's microprocessors is expected to double every 2 years, as it has in the past. By the end of this decade desktop computers will be more powerful than today's supercomputers, and pocket-size computers will not be far behind, overtaking the market for laptops. The development of "nanotechnology" will result in microprocessor chips down to macromolecule size. Some observers suggest that twenty-first-century personal computers will be very personal, indeed, embedded in our clothing, our eyeglasses, or our jewelry. The future is well beyond our imagination.

Similar developments are foreseen in other aspects of the communication-information industry. Decades ago we marveled at communications satellites that brought distant news events to our living room television set the instant they took place. Television diplomacy has challenged the secrecy of the embassy. National politics and international conflicts are visible, even in those countries that seek to control what their citizens can see or learn. Today our access to foreign television programs is no longer limited to news; through direct satellite broadcasting, television viewing has become a truly global affair, with signals penetrating the borders of rival, even hostile nations.

For the past 50 years, the household communications environment has been controlled by outside forces: broadcast television, the insistent and disconcerting phone call at the wrong time, and the plague of wrong numbers or abusive callers. We have dinner after the evening news, go to sleep after the late night news, or lose sleep to watch a late-night talk show. Families now want to control their household communications environment.

Information technologies abound in American homes, especially among young families, with or without children. More than 95% of these families have a VCR; more than one-third have a personal computer, and, of these, almost one-fifth communicate or access databases remotely; and there are answering machines in 50% of these young households. These families purchase many telephone devices and services that enable them to control electronic access to them, to enhance their communications capability, including the ability to conference, to forward calls to another number, and so on. New technologies such as voice mail, the videophone, personal communications, database access, and caller identification are likely to be favorably received.

This concentration of information services and devices seeks to recreate the separation of family life from civil life, and return control to the individual and the family. Further, these technologies offer the ability to manage information consumption and enhance information production. There are, however, troublesome signs that raise doubts about the arrival of a knowledge- or information-based society. By mid-1991 the impressive growth of the U.S. computer industry, the world leader, turned sour, experiencing its worst slump since the mid-1980s. Price cutting, a sure sign of a maturing industry, put the squeeze on profit margins. Mergers, bankruptcies, and employee layoffs followed. The $500-billion world information industry, from media to software to telecommunications, has been in its biggest slump ever. No longer do we see growth rates of 20% per year; in recent years the rate has been in the neighborhood of 6% or less. While this might well have been expected after the dramatic growth of the industry, the dynamic expansion in the production of information during the previous years, and the general business slowdown throughout the world, a more serious cloud hovered on the horizon. The consumption of information has not kept pace with its production. Information production appears to be growing at a rate of more than 10% per year, while information consumption has lagged behind at about 3% or 4% per year. Estimating the production and consumption of information is a tricky business, but even if it is only an indication of trends, it is worth thinking about seriously.

Whatever happened to the paperless society that was supposed to become real in the 1980s? Instead we see a proliferation of paper, photocopied and faxed. Electronic libraries and newspapers feeding electronic and instant information services have fallen by the wayside, as major publishers and banks, such as McGraw-Hill, Knight-Ridder and Citibank, have seen their multimillion-dollar investments go up in smoke. A third of the U.S. GNP of $5.5 trillion is in ideas and information, but their producers are working no more productively than they were 30 or more years ago. White-collar productivity seems to have stagnated while blue-collar productivity continues to increase. In the information society the skilled white-collar workers are supposed set the productivity pace.

If there is a growing gap between the production and consumption of information there is, perhaps, an even greater gap between what have come to be known as the information rich and the information poor. Information technology and modern telecommunications raised renewed hopes for enhancing national development. Development information replaced development communications as the mechanism for stimulating growth in the developing and newly industrializing countries. Whether development information can be a catalyst for development is a moot point in many countries, where reliable telephone or even telegraph communications are rarely available, and where computers are only in the dreams of young people returning from studying in advanced countries. Plagued by barriers of poverty, poor health, low life expectancy, illiteracy, and little access to tertiary education, emerging countries must compete with advanced countries in a highly competitive global marketplace. What does the information society mean to them? Economic growth in the least-developed nations of the world has stagnated or has been increasing very, very slowly. The gap between the developed and lesser-developed nations continues to widen annually. Can these Third World nations ever catch up?

All is not serene in those nations that pride themselves on being information societies. Information technology and modern telecommunications have made global aggregation of firms possible, have made the dream of worldwide monopoly capitalism a reality. For some this means greater market power and wealth, for others it means poverty and the loss of jobs, for some nations perhaps the loss of economic sovereignty. Despite early predictions that information workers would be riding high in an information economy, they are often the first to lose their jobs as firms consolidate their activities and relocate work, made less valuable by information technology, to low-wage-rate countries. In addition to white-collar and blue-collar workers there are pink-collar workers whose tasks have been downgraded as a result of the application of information technology. Growth of GNP, even in the highly industrialized and informationalized nations, has been quite slow. The United States, perhaps the premier example of an information society, has experienced relatively low rates of growth of Gross National Product, about 3.0% per year between 1980 and 1988 (4.4% for 1987-1988), but that has rapidly fallen to about 2% per year for 1989-1991 and less than 1% for 1991-1992.

Information technology and telecommunications make aggregation feasible, and aggregation of economic activity leads to higher profits and greater market power on a global scale. The Soviet empire, challenged and infiltrated by global television and the personal computer, has crumbled, only to be replaced by renewed nationalism and religious and racial intolerance recalling the years before World War I. It seems that the more we go global, the more likely we are to be plagued by communalism and nationalism.

It is time to "come down to earth," to explain just what the information society has been so far and what it promises to be, just what it has meant to society and what it is likely to mean for society in the future. Too frequently, the term *technology* means complexity and expense, despite how much more pleasant our life has become because of modern technology. And just as frequently technology is seen as the panacea for all our ills. Complicating the public's concern about technology is the sudden emergence of information as a technology, information that we have taken for granted for so long. After all, we consume information when we talk to our family and friends, read newspapers, and pay attention to radio and television broadcasts. Why, then, have information, information technology, and the information economy and society become so visible and assumed so much importance in our daily lives?

To answer these questions and provide a guide to understanding the nature of the information society and economy, we take a retrospective view to see where we have been and what have been the consequences of the policies made. We examine why some goals have been achieved and others have not. Recognizing that the enthusiasm for radical change in the highly industrialized world has spilled over into the newly industrialized nations and to the Third World, we explore the consequences for these nations.

It has been claimed that modern information technology and telecommunications have heralded a new society and a new man and woman, that man's expectations of the ultimate improvability of man can be realized. The Industrial Revolution has been replaced, we are told, by the information revolution, but with none of the disbenefits of the former. Has a global economy, caught in the web of modern telecommunications and information technology, emerged? And what has been the impact on both the industrializing and industrialized nations? In particular, what has been the impact of informatization on the individual, and have we learned from our experience in the Industrial Revolution over the past 200 or more years to utilize new technologies more efficiently, effectively, humanely, and ethically?

Drawing on information from pilot schemes for business and the home which have been accomplished in Japan, Singapore, Taiwan, Malaysia, and other Southeast Asian nations, as well as in West Germany, and the services now marketed in the United Kingdom, France, and the United States, we examine the projections made by promoters and detractors, by enthusiasts and critics. This volume will determine the status and consequences of the information revolution and look for the information society in those nations that have, over the past 20 years, announced policies for informatization and have undertaken specific programs to achieve informatization. We examine the highly developed nations, the industrializing "tigers" in the Far East and other industrializing countries, and the emerging nations. The objective of this work is to provide a realistic estimate of where we stand vis-à-vis the forecasts that have been made over the past 20 years.

This is an exceptionally appropriate time to revisit the claims that have been made for the emerging information society. Personal computers have been available in almost every industrialized country and in many newly emerging nations. Many pilot schemes aimed at business and the home have been accomplished and information services have been marketed for more than 10 years. In the United States information services and networks have been available in the marketplace for more than 20 years. Other nations are in various stages of adopting technology and in reevaluating past policies before creating new economic and social development policies. Educators, scientists, and engineers trained during this era have now entered the schools and universities, business and industry, and are pioneering the utilization of the network marketplace and paving the way for their successors. Are we witnessing the dawning of a new age, the information age, economy, or society? Jean Voge, an astute observer of the information scene, calls the information society a network for a crumbling pyramid. Are we on the delicate cusp of this new age, or are we witnessing an evolutionary phase of the ongoing Industrial Revolution?

2

Information Technology, the Information Society, and the Economy

The coming of the information society was signaled by the growth of an information sector in the economy, much as Tadeo Umesao forecast in 1963. The growth of this sector is evident in the kinds of work we do and what we do with most of our waking hours. Our work, to a large degree, defines our lives and our society. It behooves us to examine this information society in more detail before embarking on determining how far we are along in this transformation.

Improvement Ideologies and the Information Society

The information society was dimly perceived in the early writings of observers in Japan, who often waxed philosophical about a new world in which material values were to be replaced by more spiritual ones. In the West the conceptual notions of a new society that would emerge after the full flowering of the industrial society, just as that society emerged from the agricultural one that preceded, followed from the idea of progress much as the idea of development did. In the 1960s and 1970s there were several versions of how the continuation of the Industrial Revolution to its natural and historical conclusion would lead to a postindustrial society. One image of the postindustrial society was to be the information society.

There was little doubt that this transformation reflected human progress, and it was seen as a natural evolution for society that grew out of various improvement ideologies. We examine the improvement ideologies that constitute several versions of this postindustrial society and how the important concept of the information society has been formulated.

There were two conceptual paths toward the idea of an information society. One path is exemplified by the writings of Rolf Dahrendorf, Daniel Bell, Jacques Ellul, and others, who sought to relate the increasing sophistication of technology and planning to the emergence of a new society. Rostow reflected on this new society, using the analogy of the Buddenbrooks dynamics in Thomas Mann's novel of three generations: "The first sought money; the second, born to money, sought social and civic positions; the third, born in comfort and social prestige, looked to the life of music" (Rostow, 1961, p. 150). Another path was more directly related to the growing importance of information- or knowledge-based industries being observed by Umesao and Masuda in Japan, and Machlup and Porat in the United States.

Dahrendorf, Bell, and Ellul preached ideologies of improvement. Dahrendorf focused his attention on the societal goal of liberty as being the appropriate next step after material needs have been satisfied (Dahrendorf, 1975, p. 81). Only in a world in which material goals have been met could it be possible for the search for liberty to be undertaken without incurring injustices in the allocation of resources. Dahrendorf's idea of liberty is not liberty for the poor to live in great wealth, but rather a society freed from concentration on the material, a society that recognizes the feasibility of the pursuit of liberty and of choices for alternative life-styles. Dahrendorf recognizes the importance of expanding economic growth in order to meet material needs, but also that the means for improving society are political, "public, general, and open. . . . This, then, is what the improving society is all about; a new lease of life for men boxed up in the unnecessary cubicles of an inherited division of labor, based on an economy of good husbandry and brought about by a political organization in which the revolt of the individual is reconciled with the need for recognizing both the reality of organization and the utility of wider spaces" (Dahrendorf, p. 81). Dahrendorf argues that economic growth is necessary to cope with problems of poverty and inequality, of food scarcity, and of pollution; but economic growth cannot be the center of our attention if our goal is to improve society by assuring the "new liberty." His arguments are as applicable to industrialized nations, in which there are pockets of poverty, as to developing nations.

Daniel Bell's concept of the postindustrial society suggested that, unlike Rostow's stages of growth thesis in which economic growth is the "axial principal," in a postindustrial society the axial principle is the acquisition and codification of theoretical knowledge. Power resides in the possession and in the possessors of that knowledge (Bell, 1973, pp. 18-20).

Following industrialization there would emerge a society "organized around knowledge for the purpose of social control and the directing of innovation and change" (Bell, 1973, p. 20). Social control, in Bell's terms, calls for more conscious decision making precisely because of the awareness of the importance of information and knowledge. Because the chief problem of social choice is the inability to order the preferences of individuals, this ordering can only take place through bargaining between groups. But in order to bargain effectively, one needs to know social benefits and social costs, and this requires information and knowledge. Bell continued with his notion of the dominance of the "sociologizing mode" over the "economizing mode" as a criterion for decision making: "The 'economizing' mode is oriented to functional efficiency and the management of things (and men treated as things). The 'sociologizing' mode establishes broader social criteria, but it necessarily involves the loss of efficiency, the reduction of production and other costs that follow the introduction of non- economic values" (pp. 42-43).

Bell (1973) observed the significance of the postindustrial society in that:

1. It strengthens the role of science and cognitive values as a basic institutional necessity of the society;
2. By making decisions more technical it brings the scientist or economist more directly into the political process;
3. By deepening existing tendencies toward the bureaucratization of intellectual work it creates a set of strains for the traditional definitions of intellectual pursuits and values; and

4. By creating and extending a technical intelligentsia, it raises crucial questions about the relation of the technical to the literary intellectual. (p. 43)

The change from an industrial to a postindustrial society will be observable in the gradual transformation of the industrial sector into the service sector. We shall see a growing percentage of white-collar workers, especially of professional and technical employment, in the work force. Further, we shall observe the planning of technology and the rise of an "intellectual technology," by which he means the development of problem-solving rules that may be embodied in a computer program, or sets of instructions based on statistics or mathematical formulas (p. 29). The most significant occupational categories will be the professions, engineers, technicians, and scientists. The society is dependent on information and abstract analysis for its maintenance; its critical activity is the codification and assimilation of knowledge; and the crucial power variable is the control of knowledge. A point made by Bell is that the revolutions in science and technology required by the postindustrial society cannot be led by the working class, and that a new society will emerge in which the dominance of the professional and technical classes will prevail. There will be, says Bell, a highly trained elite who will be the established ruling class. It is this new ruling class that will lead the way toward social development and social improvement.[1]

Bell (1973) approached a definition of an information or knowledge sector but preferred to use more traditional terms, as shown in Table 2.1. However, he did not label the postindustrial society as an information- or knowledge-based society. "The question has been asked why I have called this speculative concept the 'post-industrial' society, rather than the knowledge society, or the information society, or the professional society. . . . In Western society we are in the midst of a . . . change in which old relations, existing power structures . . . are being rapidly eroded. . . . What the new social forms will be like is not completely clear" (p. xiv). Bell's work falls clearly within the tradition of the improvement theorists.

While Jacques Ellul cannot be considered in the mainstream of improvement philosophers, his important work, *The Technological Society* (Ellul, 1964) formulates a comprehensive social philosophy of our technical society, one that might very well have inspired Bell's postindustrial society as rooted in an "intellectual technology." For Ellul, *technique* is much more than a technology or a group of technologies. It is an attitude of mind that Ellul describes by quoting Harold Lasswell's

Table 2.1 The Economic Sector

Tertiary
Transportation
Utilities
Quaternary
Trade
Finance
Insurance
Real Estate
Quinary
Health
Education
Research
Government
Recreation

SOURCE: Adapted from *The Coming of Post Industrial Society* (p. 117) by D. Bell, 1973, New York: Basic Books.

definition of technique: "The ensemble of practices by which one uses available resources in order to achieve certain valued ends" (p. 18). We are entering, writes Ellul, a world in which our actions will be preceded by planning for well-defined goals for which we shall assemble an "ensemble of means" or "technique" designed to achieve, in an optimal manner, the goals we have carefully planned for. No longer will man be divided in his relation to technique, but man and technique will be molded into one in order to live in this technological society. Ellul warns that this is not all to the good; a society without spiritual values is an empty one. The technological society will have to find ways to retrieve its humanity without losing the benefits of the wise use of technology.

Here, then, are three paradigms of progress: the new liberty, the postindustrial society, and the technological society. In 1972, following the studies begun in the 1960s, the Japan Computer Usage Development Institute (JACUDI) announced an ambitious plan to establish information/databases of value to industry and individuals, and introduce computer education and management information systems in Japan. Masuda (1981) compiled this information in his *The Information Society as Post Industrial Society*.

In his view of an information society, Masuda finds a marriage between the imperatives of progress and the maintenance of human values. He proposes an information society in which information values, rather than material values, are the driving force. He points to economic factors that constitute this society: universally available information at affordable cost, and quantity and quality of information with facilities for the distribution of the stocks and flows of this information. As a result information communities on a human scale, participatory democracy, and the spirit of globalism would emerge. While he and other Japanese scholars may have painted a utopian picture, Masuda ventured beyond economics and explored social and cultural changes, pointing to goals for achieving greater individual self-actualization and harmonious relationships among people. He seeks a bridge between Bell's sociologizing and economizing modes, a bridge that will achieve what Ellul believes is necessary: technology with a human face. Masuda suggests that the information society is that bridge.

For Porat and Rubin, in the United States, it was the shifting roles of the labor force that defined an information society. A new kind of worker is required as a society evolves from one that produces agricultural and manufactured products to one that produces and distributes knowledge. Porat argued that the United States had become an information society because the mix of jobs and products had been shifting toward information-related activities for more than 40 years, beginning in the early 1940s. Activities that produced information as end products had been growing faster than agriculture and manufacturing, and there were more people engaged in information work of one form or another than there were in manufacturing, agriculture, or the delivery of services (Porat & Rubin, 1977).

Speculations on the Consequences of the Coming of the Information Society

The information society does not come cost-free; there are consequences. The first comprehensive work to recognize that information technology would profoundly affect society was the Nora-Minc study, performed at the request of the President of France and published in 1980 (Nora & Minc, 1980). For the first time the term *informatisation* (informatization) was used to denote a process of change leading to an information society, a process that does not simply involve progress in telematics, that is, interconnection between computer and telecommunication systems, but also one that "alters the entire nervous system of social organizations." Nora and Minc wrote that proactive government policies are necessary to ensure that this progress will take place for the betterment of the nation and its people. For if France "does not respond effectively to the serious new challenges she faces, her internal tensions will deprive her of the ability to control her fate." These new challenges were "the increasing computerization of society" (in the resounding French, *l'informatisation de la societé*), which could bring about "changes for the better or for the worse," depending upon the policies France chooses for itself (p. 3).

Nora and Minc unequivocally stated that information technology (telematique) would accelerate the emergence of a very highly productive society with "less but more effective work and jobs very different from those imposed by industrial life" (p. 126). With the changing nature of work would inevitably come questions about the value of work. A wide gulf would appear between those who perform high-technology, intellectually challenging work, and a nonprofessional class who will have fewer, lower paying, routine tasks. Further, the structure of organizations would necessarily be altered to take advantage of the productivity benefits information and information technology offers, as would the roles of managers and management tasks. When knowledge becomes the engine of growth, there will be significant social and economic changes, comparable to those that took place when agriculture was replaced by manufacturing as the engine of growth. The Nora and Minc report became a best-seller and attracted widespread attention in Europe. It did not, however, offer a precise definition of an information society. It presented a view of an information society as one in which the production, distribution, and consumption of knowledge and information are the driving forces for change. In this it was similar to the earlier work of Masuda and Umasao as well as Bell. The real point of departure between this work and other works before and since was in its emphasis on the degree and consequences of societal change and the cost of not choosing the path toward informatization.

To the technological utopians the new society would be totally different from the past in economic structure, life-styles, and personal value orientation (Masuda, 1981). Our society will be free from pollution and traffic jams because a majority of the population will stay at home to work and receive education. As the computer frees human beings from all routine jobs, more time will be allowed for creative work and spiritual cultivation. Broad access to information will help bring about participatory democracy and a perfect market; redefine the core-peripheral relationship within either an organization or a nation, and at the global level; and establish harmony among individuals, society, and national groups.

The pessimists, on the other hand, see no major structural changes to justify a claim for a historical or societal discontinuity (e.g., Kumar, 1978; Williams, 1983). Competition for profit will persist, accompanied by continuing, even increasing alienation in the workplace, and surveillance by the bureaucracy will only revive painful memories of the industrial age (Kumar, 1978, p. 231). They see the coming of a dark age where information and information technology only serve to benefit the rich, such as multinational giants, for more profit exploitation, and the powerful for tighter control over individuals. As a result the persistent gap between the haves and have-nots will widen while problems, such as the invasion and erosion of privacy and of national sovereignty, will continue to worsen (Lyon, 1988, pp. 21-42).

As in many theoretical debates, differences between the utopians and the pessimists are not likely to be resolved; both remain "captives of their value system" (Hammelink, 1983, p. 76). Underlying their arguments, however, are three shared key elements: technology, economic growth, and social change, which, by no coincidence, also formed the core concepts of most development theories. Clearly, these two bodies of theories have different perspectives and areas of concern, that is, studies of the information society have focused on the role of information and knowledge and changes taking place in industrialized nations, while development theories have attempted to grapple with the formula that would lead to a better life for people in developing nations. But with an increasing number of developing nations making informatization a necessary step to achieving development, we can no longer afford to discuss social changes without paying attention to informatization. Our understanding of the significance of informatization would be seriously limited if we turn away from the situation outside the industrialized world. To date, theories on information society are still being tested, but development theories have already undergone considerable revisions and modifications. What we have learned from these modifications should offer important insights into what we foresee in the future for informatization.

The Many Meanings of Development

Development is a complex process that encompasses economic, social, and political growth. Development is often a painful process precisely because it affects people's attitudes and beliefs. We examine the meanings of development as a prelude to our discussion of how and why information is now seen as a primary agent for stimulating national development.

The literature of development is vast; there are few economists of note who have not examined the mystery of national development. Economists' interest in development were spurred at the end of World War II, with the end of traditional colonialism. While other forms of colonialism soon emerged, massive postwar assistance by the United States, in particular, called for some guidance to ensure that the money would be well spent. Several theories of development were proposed: a theory that drew upon historical experience to formulate a linear process of growth; one that placed structural reform at the top of the list for success; another that recognized that while old-style empire colonialism was dead, a new form of colonialism fostered by capitalism had taken its place and had to be dealt with to promote development among the less fortunate nations; and most recently, a theory that argues that a return to traditional market economics will solve the development problems of the developing nations and stimulate economic growth in the more developed nations. We shall discuss each of these.[2]

Following this summary we shall discuss the idea of development communications: not a theory of development, but, as its proponents have argued, a necessary concomitant of the development process. Communications and communications technology are perceived as agents of economic, social, and political change. From this has comes the more recent notion that informatization should be perceived as an agent of change, a powerful force for development.

The Stages of Growth

The stages of growth thesis suggests that the advanced countries have all experienced a series of steps or stages through which all countries must proceed. "It is possible to identify all societies, in their economic dimensions, as lying within one of four categories: the traditional society, pre-conditions for take-off into self-sustaining growth, the drive to maturity, and the age of high mass consumption."[3]

In this essentially economic model, a mixture of savings, investment, and foreign aid in the right quantities was necessary to enable the developing countries to move along the path the more developed nations had traversed in the past. Take-off would occur if domestic and foreign savings were mobilized in order to generate investment and, thereby, accelerate economic growth.

However, this model does not seem to work in many nations, and it is quite obvious why. Economic growth is a necessary but not sufficient condition for development. Those countries to which the model applied, as in Europe following World War II, possessed political and social institutions and structures, Western attitudes toward progress, well-trained and educated manpower, and the ability to create an efficient government, all of which enabled these nations to convert their savings to investment, leading to increased output. But not all nations are blessed with these prerequisites, and even if so blessed, face very uncertain development paths. With the rising level of global economics and politics, Third World nations are now an integral part of a complex international system, and external forces can often nullify internal development plans, no matter how well-intentioned. Thus, a developing nation can very well be on a traditional path toward development, effectively using foreign assistance and maintaining a reasonable degree of political and even economic independence, only to be shaken from this path by an economic downturn in a powerful nation that extends recessionary trends throughout the world.

Structural Change:
A Necessary (and Sufficient?) Condition for Growth

The argument for this model is that in developing nations there are a heavy emphasis on traditional subsistence agriculture and a large agricultural sector. The underdeveloped economy consists of an overpopulated rural sector, characterized by low productivity, and a more productive urban industrial sector. For development to occur, however, there must be a more modern, diverse, and urbanized manufacturing and service economy. Unless labor is transferred from the rural sector while the more modern urban sector continues to increase its productivity, development will not occur. As in the historical model, emphasis is on economic factors, the rate of industrial investment and capital accumulation in the modern sector, as well as on the degree to which technological developments are adopted.

This model assumes that labor and capital transferred from the agricultural sector are invested in the industrializing sector, and that the faster this is done, the faster the rate of development. But what if the industrial sector adopts modern technology and invests in labor-saving capital equipment, or seeks more profitable investments overseas, as is becoming more likely in the global economy? The consequences are that the nation's productivity and output increase but employment does not, or there is a flight of capital out of the country, decreasing internal investment that should have been used to increase output and improve the standard of living.

This model also assumes that there is both a surplus of labor in the rural sector and full employment in the urban sector. In fact, the reverse has been the case, with urban unemployment rising as rural people flock to the cities in search of jobs and social services. It is not at all clear that there is a labor surplus in the rural areas. In many developing nations, large information and service sectors may hide the level of real unemployment in the urban sector, as is the case in Egypt and Thailand, where this labor is absorbed by the government and does not contribute to the productivity of the nation.[4]

With the increasing globalization of the world economy and the ease with which labor and capital can move around the world, one might expect a transfer of labor and capital from the traditional sector to a modernizing industrial sector leading to economic growth. However, this has not occurred in many developing countries. Economic growth is a necessary but not sufficient condition for development. Structural change, the shift to a more balanced economy in which an agricultural sector and a diverse manufacturing sector are important factors in the development process. For development to proceed, there must also be a trained and educated work force, an effective government, public investments in basic infrastructure, communications, and transportation, as well as a positive attitude toward progress.

The Global Economy Creates
Third World Dependency and Underdevelopment

There was growing dissatisfaction with the stages of growth and structural reform models during the 1970s. There was also growing awareness of the emerging global economy and the economic colonialism that was emerging, made evident by the increasing dependency of the developing nations on the more highly developed nations. The underdeveloped nations were on the periphery of the world economy, either because the industrialized nations believed this was necessary for the maintenance of their continuing growth as capitalistic societies or because of historical precedent. Dominance of the highly developed nations over the Third World nations hindered their development.

In this model, underdevelopment is seen as externally produced. The only way to resolve this dilemma is not reform of the existing international economic system, but a radical overhaul of international imbalances and fundamental institutional and economic reforms, domestically and internationally, to equalize the vast differences between the developed and the developing nations. Dramatically increased assistance to these nations from the wealthier nations, and in extreme cases, outright appropriation of privately owned assets in the developing countries leading to government ownership of these assets, were necessary.

The failure of the command economies of the Marxist countries in Eastern Europe in the late 1980s has tempered enthusiasm for this model of development. This is not to say that there is no validity to the historical arguments on which this model is based. Indeed, the developing nations' lack of resources and their increasing difficulties in finding a niche in the competitive global markets makes it increasingly clear that some of the recommendations derived from this model should, in fact, be adopted to spark development.

Is the Free Market Sufficient for Development and Economic Growth?

The emergence of conservative governments in the United States, the United Kingdom, and West Germany, in the 1980s, shifted emphasis away from public ownership to privatization, to supply side economics, and to either liberalizing or outright repeal of business regulations. The major development assistance organizations, such as the World Bank and the International Monetary Fund, with encouragement from the powerful nations now moving toward neoclassical market economics, encouraged developing nations to move in the same direction.

Underdevelopment results from poor resource allocation due to incorrect pricing policies and too much government intervention. What is needed is the promotion of free markets and laissez-faire economics and government hands-off policies that would allow Adam Smith's "invisible hand" to work. This will lead to more rational pricing and, consequently, more efficient allocation of resources.

However, not all developing nations have knowledge of markets or pricing, and may be more closely related to barter economies than money economies. They do not have the same social values as nations that have accepted markets as the primary means for determining social priorities. Their institutional and political structures are not suited to the development of markets. Because they have been centrally planned economies for so long, they have not developed the skills a free market economy requires for its effective operation. Again, we find that development is more than economic growth. Development requires attitudinal changes, cultural adaptation, a trained and educated work force, and a political structure that is willing to take the inherent risks that development inevitably requires.

Development Communications as an Agent of Social and Political Reform

When a group of scholars, representing the psychological and social sciences, met at the East-West Center in Honolulu in 1964 to discuss the uses of communications in economic and social development, it was at the high point of the period of interest in national development. We examine the arguments they set forth in some detail because they are the origin of today's oft-stated notion that information or informatization is an important determinant of development.

It may have been because of dissatisfaction with the outcome of economic development in the 1950s that these scholars looked toward the miracle of electronic communications as a means for stimulating growth in the lesser developed countries. And, indeed, communications technology appeared to have promise. The transistor emerged from the laboratory and rapidly appeared in the far-flung corners of the world as the transistor radio. There seemed to be no limit to where these radios could be found: in the hands of camel-riding Bedouins in the Arabian Desert, accompanying African laborers as they worked on roads, and on the tractors of farmers in the wheat fields of the United States and the collective farms of the Soviet Union. Television was rapidly becoming a household appliance in the developed nations, and almost every developing country was debating not whether but how they should introduce television with its power to inform, persuade, and educate, and thereby facilitate development.

In 1964 it was argued that the mass media is an important agent of change, that the mass media—the press and radio and later television—could be instrumental in motivating those members of the underdeveloped community who were not tradition-bound to improve their lot. The mass media could show these people the world outside their limited horizon, allowing them to project themselves into what might be and encouraging personal change by raising their level of expectation. The mass media were seen to be an important handmaiden to the "take-off" economic model proposed by Rostow. Hand in hand, they could make for national development. Government could harness these rising expectations to set and, indeed, achieve economic as well as social goals along the way to development. The steps between rising expectations and economic growth were unspecified. Nevertheless, it was assumed by many that, somehow, once having raised these expectations, increasing GNP and GNP/capita would be achieved.

Development communications, the intersection of the communications and the economic and social sciences, came to the Third World as an important component of the stages of development model proposed at that time. Daniel Lerner suggested a chain of hypotheses: that urbanization increases literacy, literacy increases mass media consumption, and mass media consumption increases electoral participation—all of which are necessary for development to occur. Subsequently, he sharpened his argument: Urbanization increases literacy, literacy increases mass media consumption and, in turn, mass media consumption increases literacy, and both literacy and mass media consumption increase electoral participation (Lerner, 1958). Two variations of these theories have been tested: (1) Urbanization increases both literacy and media consumption, literacy increases media consumption, and media consumption increases political participation and (2) urbanization increases literacy, literacy increases media consumption, and literacy and media consumption increase political participation (Alker, 1966).

Statistical fits were rare and did not indicate what causes what, even when time-lagged: That is, if literacy increased for a period of 5 years, did it follow that during the next 5 years there was an increase in political participation? Another analysis found a somewhat better correlation using 10-year lags and showing a fit to the following statement of the model chain: Communication causes urbanization, education, and development; urbanization causes education; and education causes communications and development (Windham, 1970).

Daniel Lerner's research, and the writings of Wilbur Schramm, helped launch the belief that if "Third World countries would only invest in communication infrastructure and extend the reach of mass media, the mind set that had, for centuries, hampered entrepreneurial activity within their societies would be worn down and they would be able to begin the long and arduous climb towards development" (Jayaweera & Amnugama, 1987, p. 26).

The central beliefs in this development model may be summarized as follows:

1. Development is essentially the maximizing of goods and services available to a given society and it is quantifiable.

2. The developing world is distinguished from the developed world by the paucity of these goods and services.

3. One of the main impediments to the developing world's increasing its stock of goods and service is the consciousness of its people. Locked within their own experiences they have no way of knowing what is available to them. If they could be made aware of the gains made in other parts of the world, they would have a different perception of what they could become. They would abandon their traditional ways and habits and refuse to be satisfied with producing only for their immediate needs and would produce a surplus that would bring them and their society additional income, which would then enable them to generate greater earnings, more production, more savings, more investments, more jobs, more demand, and so on.

4. The quickest and most effective way of bringing about this change of consciousness was the application of "technology-based" communications, principally radio and, in time, television. Literacy is not required; images are created that promote "psychic mobility"; and messages concerning health, education, farming methods, and more are delivered.

Nations, both developed and underdeveloped, rapidly entered the broadcast era, constructing broadcast infrastructures and investing in programming. But the rich became richer, and the poor poorer. The development that did occur was soon seen as undesirable. Critics of the model argued that rising expectations would lead to rising frustrations as nations could not satisfy consumer wants without meeting production needs. The outcome would either be the fall of governments or the imposition of highly restrictive measures to limit consumption. Furthermore, the model did not take into account the cultural differences among nations. Not every nation would be satisfied with the kinds of wants shown by the mass media. The mass media frequently presented messages and images that were foreign and unwanted by the developed nations. The cost of original programming was high, and programs were imported from nations that had had television for some time, such as the United States, the United Kingdom, and France.

There were other models of development that responded more appropriately to these cultural differences. To conceive of development simply as maximizing goods and services was inadequate, for development was more than a process of acquisition of goods and services. Development requires a fair and just distribution of economic product and political participation. The principal impediment to development in the developing world was not lack of communications but the prevalence of inequitable economic, social, and political structures, both national and international. What was needed was to liberate the people from these structures. Finally, mass communications simply tended to replicate the individualism and acquisitiveness common to capitalistic societies in the Third World. This was not ideologically or morally desirable. Clearly, these critics were influenced by the dependency model of underdevelopment discussed above.

Development communications was linked to the stages of growth model, one that had worked in the Western countries and in Japan and was expected to do the same in the rest of Asia, Africa, and Latin America. While few people challenged this model seriously, in 1975 the condition of a large part of the developing world was not much better than in 1964.

Concern for the quality of life replaced the single-minded pursuit of economic goals. Many became suspicious of technology and large-scale industrialization, and the ideas of "small is beautiful" and of appropriate technology gained favor (Schumacher, 1975). It was felt that development should be focused on self-help and appropriate technology, and it would be best for the developing nations to isolate themselves from the developed world and plan their own routes to development. China, with its backyard steel furnaces, Tanzania with its extensive self-help programs, and several other nations in the Communist orbit were given as examples of this development model. Balanced growth, emphasizing the mobilization of human and social resources in addition to economic resources, was required. And the cultural base of society was too important to be left unattended, for this determines the pace and direction of development. A new approach to Third World development emerged:

1. Third World societies should aim to satisfy basic needs rather than seek rapid modernization.
2. Fundamental reforms in the structures of international trade and monetary institutions are necessary.

3. Structural reforms within the Third World societies must take place, including land reform, increased opportunities for political participation, decentralization of planning, and the creation of adequate credit institutions.

4. Reliance on foreign aid and capital-intensive technology must give way to self-reliance and appropriate technology, followed by a reduced bias for manufacturing and an increased emphasis on agriculture, and

5. Development must be within the framework of existing cultures and customs.

Schumacher's world of the beautifully small was a pleasant and nostalgic dream; while he demanded a more balanced adoption of technology, it was, essentially, an anti-technological view. In a world of high tension between the haves and the have-nots, not only among nations but within nations as well, this presented the prospect that the past need not be replaced by an entirely unknown future. Nations as well as people only remember the good rather than the bad, are comfortable with the certain rather than the uncertain, and so the past is always seen as preferable to the future. But this is not so. Poverty, backwardness, ill health, illiteracy, lack of opportunity, and dictatorial governments are not nostalgically sought after. In any case, in a world in which the idea of progress has taken a solid hold on men's minds, what choices do the poor nations have but to pursue technological change? Indeed, what choices do the industrialized nations have but also to pursue technological change and economic growth, and hope to do so without destroying cherished values. Dieter Senghas (1983) said it best:

> What choices do the Third World countries have? Hardly any, any for a variety of reasons. Firstly, the dominant elites of most Third World countries whether elected or not, civilian or military, are the principal local beneficiaries of this relationship (with the highly industrialized world). They are vulnerable to all manner of blandishments that accompany high-power sales drives. Secondly, it will be foolhardy and impracticable to opt out of the world-wide network of satellites, computers and digitalized telephones. No country can stay away from these networks and yet remain within the mainstream of world commerce. Thirdly, popular pressure within these countries, that is, the demand for commodities and the good life, is so rampant, that regardless of a society's capacity to afford them, governments are compelled to supply them even by resorting to external borrowings. The alternative is to be forced out of office or to increase repression. Proposals for "de-linking," "self-reliance,"

and "automatic development" are mostly conceptual fantasies that have little relevance to the realities on the ground. Though these slogans have enjoyed a high profile in the debate, they do not constitute real options. (p. 22)

For the majority of the developing nations, the Industrial Revolution was a lost opportunity, and there is little reason why they should stand by and watch another one go by. The sense of urgency for leapfrogging and catching up with the developed nations is further enhanced by the threat of the "double gap," as described by Masuda (1981):

> The industrial gap is one of productive technology . . . but the information gap means relative absence of information processing and transmission technology, to which must be added human factors of levels of intellectual development and behavioral patterns. . . . The problem is all the more serious because the information gap overlaps the industrial gap, together forming a double gap. (p. 4)

The "double gap," once formed, perpetuates inequality and deprives Third World nations of future opportunities for development, a consequence developing nations can ill afford.

Development Informatization
Replaces Development Communications

We have examined the idea of development communications in some detail because it is the forerunner of current thinking about *development informatization*. It should not be surprising that the information technologies have replaced the communications technologies as the great hope for economic growth. One purpose of this book is to examine to what extent this hope has been realized or is likely to be realized.

Today there is little doubt that technology is a significant determinant of economic growth. The technological revolution that has driven the last four decades of the twentieth century and will see us into the twenty-first century has been based upon the information technologies: computers and telecommunications. Information-based technologies are primarily software and microprocessors (the information technologies) applied to telecommunication, to manufacturing, and in offices. Because communications and computers require highly skilled workers and produce high-value products and services, both leading to a higher standard of living and to the potential for attaining a competitive niche in the global market, focusing on information technology, on informatization, is seen as a promising strategy for economic development. Industrializing nations are already investing significant portions of their limited resources in information technology. In Thailand, Taiwan, and the Philippines, a modern telecommunications infrastructure is among the highest priorities in their development plans. Following in the footsteps of India and Indonesia, many are embarking on national satellite communications projects.[5]

When the United Nations designated 1983 as World Communications Year, the World Bank and International Monetary Fund joined the efforts by publishing several reports examining the roles played by telecommunications and information technology in development. These reports further encouraged policymakers to look to information technology as an important contributor to economic growth. Additional studies reported significant benefits from investments in telecommunications, which gave further impetus to planners to invest in information technology and telecommunications, in spite of the high cost of capital and the often dire need for education and social services in the developing and industrializing nations.[6]

With the failure of the development communications model still fresh in their minds, it is not at all surprising that doubts remain about yet another technological solution to economic development. There must be some middle ground between the "bandwagon approach" of most developing nation elites and technological enthusiasts, who want to join in the race to buy new information and communications technologies, and the "fortress approach" of those who want to "pull up the drawbridges and get behind the ramparts of 'self-reliance' " (Hamelink, 1983, p. 73). Information technology cannot be ignored today, any more than the roads and railways could be ignored in the past.

Why Information and Information Technology Cannot Be Ignored

Economic growth is shaped by, and in turn shapes, the technologies that are adopted. Technology is not neutral; what technology reaches the individual, either through the market or government, and how these technologies are used are determined, in part, by the economic and political goals a nation has and by how people perceive their personal goals for progress and for achieving the good life. In traditional societies with strong religions and often fundamentalist ideologies, progress is anathema, and modern technology is often seen as a threat to established values. While nations and their powerful industrialists can attempt to impose their vision of progress, the final choice is in the hands of the consumer in a marketplace, whatever form that marketplace takes. In the last years of the 1980s the command economies of Eastern Europe confounded their leaders by becoming consumer economies. They demanded a greater choice of goods and services and voted for the progress that socialist governments had attempted to control through centralized management of technological choice, production, and investment. Modern theories of economic growth have shifted toward a laissez-faire market, minimizing the role of government and much more oriented toward consumers. However, to enter upon the first steps toward that goal, natural resources and the ability to make the best use of them is necessary. In the absence of natural resources that have value in the competitive world market, the effective utilization of labor is crucial to economic growth. Even this may not be sufficient, for this labor must be employed in the production of high-value services and products in order for nations to achieve the rising standard of living they seek. Utilization of modern technology and the development of an educational infrastructure that produces an educated and trained work force are important factors for economic growth. The large number of science and engineering students, from both developing and developed nations, attending universities in the United States attests to an awareness of the importance of technology in their nation's future. Despite periods of anti-technology revolts and Schumacher campaigns for "small is beautiful" in the past, Luddites are rarely welcomed in most nations today.

What technology to acquire and at what costs relative to other needs are questions that all nations, developing and highly industrialized, must resolve. Nations will grow only if they can parlay these technologies with skilled human resources. The rapidity with which new information technologies are being developed creates enormous pressures for continued innovation because the advantages gained are likely to be short-lived. No nation can expect to maintain a technological advantage for too long. What will count will be how well that nation can organize the market to its advantage and for how long. This requires marketing skills, organizational innovations, and an educated work force. These are the "technologies" that will count in the twenty-first century. Technology, then, should be seen not in terms of hardware or software alone but also as a way of managing, educating, and organizing.

In the highly competitive international economic environment that has emerged with the rise of the global economy, it is unlikely that any nation can expect to achieve a position of self-sufficiency or absolute comparative advantage. A developing nation cannot be the world's low-cost producer of any goods or service for long, because the domestic demands for improved standard of living and more consumer goods and services will place inexorable demands on its political leaders, who will have to satisfy these demands or be driven from office. In any case, a nation's economic and social well-being depend on its production of high-value goods and services for high-value markets.

Nations will find their comparative advantages in the special talents or endowments they can bring to the marketplace. But to begin this search requires that they achieve a level of infrastructure and technology as well as organizational skills to enable them to stimulate that search. They hope to achieve comparative advantage in industries that make intensive use of the factors they possess in abundance. Some are likely to be labor-intensive industries, as in Korea because of its large labor force. Sweden's high-quality steel industries have prospered because of its abundant iron ore with a low content of phosphorous impurities. Japan prospered because of its ability to marshal its well-educated and motivated labor force into electronics. Because communications and computers require highly skilled workers and produce high-value products that are most important to national productivity and to achieving a competitive advantage, focusing on the information technologies is seen as a promising strategy for economic development.

Technological change is pervasive and continuous: Products become increasingly differentiated and buyers' requirements more specific and varied. The increasingly competitive international market is creating the technological revolutions that reshape business structures and practices, not only in the United States but also throughout the industrialized and industrializing world. New rules for socioeconomic and political growth of the developing countries are being established. In the next century we shall recognize the wisdom of Ellul's concept of technology as a set of values leading to behavior and to a governing principal. Increasingly, products and service differentiation will be achieved through the manipulation of symbols and concretization of information in semiconductor chips and by sophisticated marketing. In the next century, many of today's technologies are expected to be global, that is, in the hands of a few, and will be purchased "off the shelf" by the many. Much of this technology will be information-based, software and microprocessors (information technology), and the world will be densely covered by many telecommunications or information networks. In this first 40 or so years of the information era, we have learned that information technology coupled with modern telecommunications can perform the coordination and communications tasks performed by a large number of middle managers, and do so very well. Furthermore, as this technology becomes available they innovate along nontraditional paths dictated by the information and telecommunications technologies. Traditionally, industrial innovation occurred along three often well-defined directions: product, process, and managerial. The revolutionary nature of the microprocessor is its influence across all of these dimensions, and innovation occurs almost simultaneously. Microprocessor-based innovation, as in the information and telecommunications technologies, affects what goods and services are produced and how these goods and services are produced and, through managerial innovations, strongly influences the nature of the organizations in which they are produced.

Information technology, and we include modern telecommunications as an information technology, may have given birth to the successor to the Industrial Revolution that emerged from England in the eighteenth century. If this is indeed so, developing nations cannot ignore information technology and the process of informatization.

There is a rather optimistic view that the effective transfer of knowledge will lead to both more rapid development and a more equitable distribution of wealth. While the world's stock of information is finite, the continued application of both present and new knowledge to those limited resources will permit future growth, perhaps unlimited future growth. But one cannot make simple claims for the relationship between information and economic growth.

It must be recognized that information and its effective or productive use are important—indeed crucial. Further, the transformation of information to knowledge is a giant leap. There are other conditions that must be met in order to stimulate national development and economic growth. For one, there must be an announced, or at least well-understood national policy that encourages the development of high-value industries, and there must be a policy that encourages constructive competition among firms, thereby promoting innovation and invention. There must be political stability and a favorable tax climate to encourage long-term investments. These are the same conditions nations must create to compete in today's global economy. There is a relationship between informatization and the global economy, and national development and economic growth; and in the remaining chapters of this book, we shall see how far nations have come in recognizing and acting on this knowledge. But first we must define what we mean by informatization and how it contributes to economic growth and national development.

Notes

1. Gershuny (1978) asks why should these elites be politically dominant, and if they were, why should they be less materialistic than the present decision makers? What grounds does Bell have for assuming that this elite will adopt the values for improving society?

2. For those wishing a more detailed discussion of the theories of development and of economic development generally, see Todaro (1989).

3. The historic approach to a theory of development was proposed by Rostow (1961).

4. How the magnitude of the information sector is related to the productivity of the industrial sector is discussed in Chapter 6.

5. In 1983 it was estimated that developing and newly industrialized nations owned but 3% of the world's synchronous (communications) satellites, but Filep (1991) notes that at least 18% of launches between 1992 and 1997 will be for regional or domestic satellites owned by Third World nations.

6. For example, small business in Kenya found that losses incurred because of poor telecommunications were, on average, 110 times greater than the cost of providing adequate telephone services. And in Egypt, 143 villages showed a 40:1 benefit to cost ratio following investments in telecommunications. When social costs are included, this ratio is 8,535:1. The World Bank estimates that, on average, the direct rate of return on investments in telecommunications is around 18%, and is much larger when returns to other industries benefiting from improved telecommunications services are included.

3

A Matter of Measurement

What We Do Defines Us and Our Society

The application of information technologies is seen every day in our lives, in the work we do and the tools we use for this work. It has become abundantly clear that so-called entry-level jobs are no longer plentiful and the need for unskilled labor is rapidly disappearing not only in the United States but also in most of the highly developed countries in the world. Look around and you will see fewer workers "bending metal" and more workers at computers and other information machines or telephones, engaged in tasks that require skill in the use of information. Increasingly, workers in advanced societies are engaged in information work, work that is more highly valued because it adds value to the products manufactured and the services marketed. No longer can a young man in Detroit, with a clean police record but no high school diploma, expect to find a job on the automobile assembly lines; these lines are now automated with robotic assemblers and controlled by computers, overseen by skilled programmers and industrial engineers.

Our young man must now have a college degree or at least a certificate of completion from an accredited vocational school, and a good grasp of mathematics and physics.

Informatization has led to structural changes in our labor force and in our economy and is shaping the future of our society and societies throughout the world. But how do we know how far we are on the way toward an information society, if there is indeed to be one? Are there measures that can help us determine the extent a society has been informatized?

Measuring a New Society

We cannot depend upon the theoretical debates between the utopians and the pessimists to assist us in this task, we must examine the "real world." We need to develop indicators that assist in defining *informatization* and the information society. Measurement, of course, does not constitute science, but measurement serves several functions that very few other methods of research can offer. By using a uniform unit of analysis, we are able to make comparisons across time and space, which give valuable information regarding the trends and patterns of development. The information generated may support or refute theories and point to new directions for future studies. For policymakers it will help decision makers design more realistic development strategies and development plans. Useful and important as measurement may be, the value of its outcome has to depend on the quality of the measurement instrument. But very often we are carried away by the findings and overlook how data were collected and how good the instruments are. It is necessary to discuss how the outcomes were derived in order to interpret them with reliability.

In this chapter we discuss how well several measures of informatization have been used in the past, as a way to better evaluate how far nations have come on the road toward informatization. In the next chapter we present the measures we use in this work.

The three parameters to our concept of informatization are Infrastructure, Economic, and Social.

Infrastructure Measures

Characteristics of a nation's infrastructure are the easiest and most direct measures to obtain. Because of this, many countries have concentrated on obtaining this data and have made the mistake of equating these measures with the status of their information societies. The key to the effective use of information is access to that information. The nation's information infrastructure is a measure of this access. National policies are created to ensure access, as in the United States, where universal telephone service, by way of telephone assistance programs operated at both federal and state levels, has become one of the very few social policies in that nation. Indeed, as competition replaces monopoly for the provision of telephone and data communications services, and as information rather than plain old telephone services becomes more important, a debate has already begun on how to preserve the principal of universal services and expansion to universal information services.[1] A systematic attempt to define an overall infrastructure index is represented by the Johoka Index.

The Johoka Index

Japan's Research Institute of Telecommunications and Economics (RITE) developed this index to determine how far Japan has moved toward being informationalized and, further, to compare the informationalization of different societies over time. The Johoka Index is composed of the following parameters for measuring an information society/economy (Ito, 1981, p. 674). We describe this index in some detail because of its similarity to our definition of informatization.

Amount of Information
    The number of telephone calls per person per year
    Newspaper circulation per 100 people
    Books published per 1,000 people
    Population density as a measure of interpersonal communication
Distribution of Communication Media
    Telephone receivers per 100 people
    Radio sets per 100 households
    Television sets per 100 households
Quality of Information Activities
    Proportion of service workers in the total population
    Proportion of students in the student age population.
Information Ratio
    Information expenditures as a proportion of total expenditures

The Information Ratio was seen as analogous to Engel's Ratio, as expressed in Engel's Law. Engel argued that as personal income increases, the percentage of expenditures for food and other necessities decreases. This ratio varies from country to country and from culture to culture. Adapting the concept to information, RITE argues that as personal or family income increases, people will spend more money for information and communication products, services, and activities such as books, television, education, concert and theater attendance, and so on. And this ratio will also vary among different societies. RITE calculated this ratio simply by subtracting all major expenses that were not clearly related to communication and information activities, such as food, clothing, and other household expenditures, and assumed that the remainder were information and communication related expenses. Figure 3.1, drawn from RITE's work, shows this ratio for 16 countries.

To compare Johoka indices between countries, the Japanese researchers divided Japan's mean score for each of the parameters of the Index by the corresponding mean value of the countries being compared, and multiplied the result by 100. Figure 3.2 provides a comparison over time of the Johoka Index for Japan and the United States, the United Kingdom, France, and West Germany (Ito, 1981, p. 679). While the United States was clearly farthest advanced toward an information society, Japan moved rapidly up this scale, overtaking France and West Germany between 1958 and 1963, but still lagging behind the United Kingdom. However, by 1968 Japan was estimated to have overtaken the United Kingdom and was behind only the United States.

The JIPDEC Index

To relate the informatization process to economic factors more directly, the Japan Information Processing and Development Center proposed the JIPDEC Index in 1986. The index is three-dimensional, composed of a *hardware ratio,* defined as the value of computer hardware in an industry, divided by the number of employees in that industry; a *software ratio,* defined as the value of software consumption over a period of 5 years, divided by the number of employees in the industry; and the *communication ratio,* defined as the information transmission capacity, divided by the number of employees in an industry (JIPDEC, 1988). The I-3 Index, as it became known, enabled the Japanese government to monitor the development of the information industry and information intensity, that is, the extent of information technology utilization in industry generally; but clearly, it was unsuit-

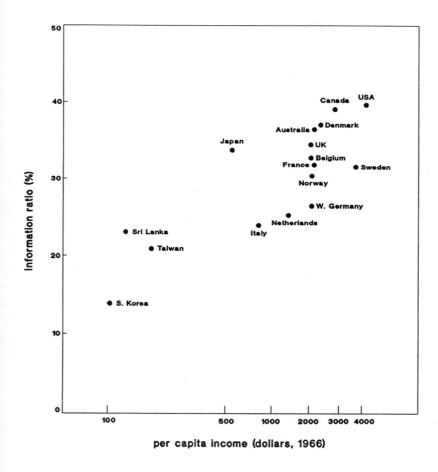

Figure 3.1. Information Ratio and Per Capita Income

SOURCE: From Introduction to Information and Communication in the Post-Industrial Society, Japan, Research Institute of Telecommunications & Economics (RITE), 1968, p. 62. Reprinted by permission.

able for monitoring the social and political dimensions, and indeed, the economic dimensions, along the nation's path toward informatization.

Economic Measures

Two general approaches have been employed to measure the economic scope of the information society: the size of the information work

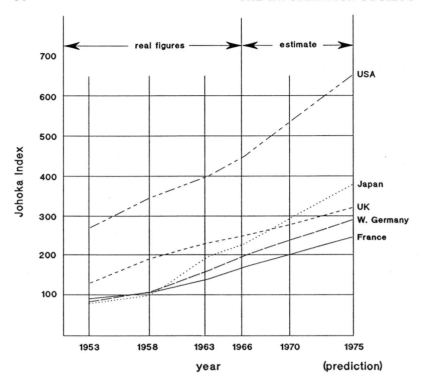

Figure 3.2. Longitudinal Trends in Johoka Indices in Five Industrial Nations

SOURCE: From Role of Telecommunications in the Post-Industrial Society, Japan, Research Institute of Telecommunications & Economics (RITE), 1970, p. 63. Reprinted by permission.

force (as a percentage of the total labor force), and its contribution to the nation's Gross Domestic Product, by sectoral analyses of labor force and contribution to GNP.

Simon Kusnetz first empirically analyzed the labor force by sectors (Kusnetz, 1957). He divided the work force into the primary sector (extractive industries such as agriculture and mining), the secondary sector (primarily manufacturing), and the tertiary sector (services). In the service sector were workers in finance, trade, transport and communications, real estate, personal service, business, domestic services, the professions, and government. Kusnetz expressed concern that we knew so little about this sector, which included people engaged in the production and distribution of knowledge as well as those engaged with major political and social decisions. He noted that this was not surprising because these activities were not large-scale and repetitive, and good data was difficult to obtain (Kusnetz, 1966).

In the early 1960s economists and social scientists began to think about a fourth occupational sector of the work force, one in which workers were engaged in knowledge- or information-intensive occupations. In an article published in 1963, Umesao predicted that the next step for industrial growth, which had progressed from agriculture to material production, would be in the realm of "spiritual production," a spiritual industry would emerge (Ito, 1981, p. 672). To Umesao, the three stages of growth could be compared to biological evolution, in which the most primitive forms of organism survive on digestive function, the more advanced forms develop muscles and live on locomotive functions, while the most advanced forms are able to prepare, plan, and control with advanced brain and nerve functions. In Umesao's analogy a spiritual industry is similar to the control function in the highest level creatures, which, through information, mass communication, telecommunication, education, cultural, and other information activities, contribute to creative and spiritual growth. Umesao introduced the term *information industries* to describe these spiritual industries (Ito, 1981, 1989). Following Umesao's 1963 publication, the term *information society* began to take hold in Japan in 1964. This led to a heated debate on the social and economic consequences of this society and its growing information industries.

Information Industries or Knowledge Industries?

At about the same time Umesao put forth his notion of information industries, halfway around the world, Fritz Machlup at Princeton University took the bold step to measure the unmeasureable: knowledge. Observing that an increasing share of the government expenditures was in activities that produced no material output, and that increasing amounts of resources were being spent by industry on similar nonmaterial outputs, Machlup sought to measure such expenditures for the production of knowledge and its importance to the nation's economy (Machlup, 1962).

To Machlup, "knowledge" is "anything that is known by somebody," and "knowledge production" is "any activity by which someone learns of something he has not known before" (p. 7). Following these definitions, five groups of knowledge-producing activities—education, research and development, media and communication, information machines, and information services—constituted what he defined as the knowledge industry. In addition, he sought to examine the size of the knowledge work force by examining the number of people holding knowledge-producing occupations. Based on data from the U.S. Census Bureau, Machlup utilized five major categories of occupations for the measurement: professional and technical workers, managers, officials and proprietors, clerical and sales workers, and craftsmen and foremen in printing trades (p. 384). A distinction was made between knowledge-producing and non-knowledge-producing workers within each category. In his analyses Machlup specifically excluded knowledge-using workers, and any work whose output is not a communication or service for knowledge transmission (p. 383).

Machlup showed that the knowledge industry and the size of its work force were responsible for a growing percentage of the GNP. His work encouraged other nations to adopt his methods but often with differing definitions of the knowledge industry and work force. In fact, most of the subsequent studies did adopt his method, only with a modified definition of the knowledge industry and its work force.

Table 3.1 (column 1) lists the knowledge industries identified by Machlup. He measured their share of the Gross National Product and their percentage of the labor force, based upon 1958 data. Machlup estimated that the knowledge industry in the United States would account for some 29% of the GNP and that slightly less than 31% of the work force would be engaged in knowledge-producing industries in 1959. Similar studies were performed in Japan, using Machlup's classifications, and it was found that Japan's knowledge industry accounted for 29.5% of the nation's GNP and 21.3% of the nation's work force in 1960.

Unlike Umesao, who conceptualized more than an economic impact on society, foreseeing significant cultural and behavioral transformations, Machlup was primarily interested in the contribution to economic growth. But their concepts converged; both saw the growing importance of essentially the same type of activities: education, communications, and the production and distribution of information.

Daniel Bell adopted a more sociological point of view in his analysis of the knowledge industries, indeed, a considerably more narrow view. He suggested that a knowledge industry should be no more than research, higher education, and the production of knowledge as an intellectual property (Bell, 1973, p. 213). Too broad a classification, including, for example, commercial printing, stationery, and office supplies

Table 3.1 Two Views of the Knowledge Industry in the United States

Industry Branches	Machlup	Government (Porat et al.)
Education		
in the home	x	
on the job	x	
in the church	x	
in the armed forces	x	
elementary & secondary	x	x
higher	x	x
commercial	x	x
federal expenditures	x	x
public libraries	x	x
implicit cost of education		
students' foregone earnings	x	
implicit rents of buildings	x	
Media of Communications		
printing & publishing	x	x
photography & phonography	x	x
stage, podium, & screen	x	x
radio and television	x	x
other advertising	x	x
telecommunications	x	x
conventions	x	
Information Machines		
printing trades	x	x
paper industries		x
musical instruments	x	
motion picture equipment	x	x
telephone & telegraph	x	x
signaling services	x	x
measuring & controlling instruments	x	x
typewriters	x	x
computers	x	x
office machines & parts	x	x
semiconductors		x
electron tubes		x
other electronic equipment		x
ink		x
photographic equipment and supplies	x	x
Information Services		
legal	x	x
engineering & architectural	x	x
accounting & auditing	x	x

continued

Table 3.1 Continued

Industry Branches	Machlup	Government (Porat et al.)
medical	x	x
securities brokers	x	x
insurance agents	x	x
real estate agents	x	x
wholesale agents	x	x
retail "information" stores		x
government activities	x	x
Other Information Activities		
research & development	x	x
construction of information buildings		x
nonprofit activities	x	x

SOURCE: From *The Knowledge Industry in the United States, 1960-1980* (pp. 8-9) by M. R. Rubin and M. T. Huber, 1986. Copyright © 1986 by Princeton University Press. And from F. Machlup, *The Production and Distribution of Knowledge in the United States* (p. 361), 1972. Copyright © 1972 by Princeton University Press. Both reprinted by permission of Princeton University Press.

in a category labeled "communication media," as Machlup did, would inevitably lead to misleading results (p. 212). This could be especially damaging to estimates of national economic growth.

Instead of trying to pinpoint "knowledge workers," Bell chose to include only two groups of professionals: scientists and engineers, and identified the economic sectors in which they are employed (p. 224). Bell's estimate of information workers was much lower than Machlup's and, if carried further, would have yielded a much smaller contribution to a nation's GNP. Both Bell and Machlup enabled one to examine changes in the information or knowledge work force over time, and Machlup provided longitudinal data over time for the contribution of knowledge industries and workers to the nation's GNP.

Both Machlup and Bell highlighted the importance of knowledge in an economy and to society. A more precise measure of a level of informatization by way of sectoral analysis, and one that would be capable of application across many countries at various levels of economic development, continued to elude economic and social planners.

In 1977 Porat and Rubin refined Machlup's work in their very comprehensive, quantitative, job-by-job study of the information economy in the United States (Porat & Rubin, 1977). Porat and Rubin elected to expand Bell's measurement to include "ancillary workers and firms who support the production and distribution of information " (p. 5). Additionally, Porat and Rubin believed that income generated by information activities, not limited to the selling price of a product as Machlup had measured it, is a better basis of measurement because it more accurately reflects the wealth generated by the information economy, as well as the contribution of these activities to the nations' economy (p. 47). Their categories not only were more comprehensive than those employed by Bell, but also reached into areas that Machlup chose to ignore, activities that supported information work such as office, school, and communication construction and building maintenance and the provision of furnishings (p. 57). They argued that while these activities may not be directly involved in the production of information, they contribute to the value of the product or service produced, and should therefore be included.

Porat and Rubin went further in their analyses to distinguish between a primary and a secondary information sector. Recognizing that an all-embracing single definition of the primary or secondary information sector would be impossible to derive, they defined the sectors by means of examples. Porat wrote that "the end product of all information service markets is knowledge. An information market enables the consumer to know something that was not known beforehand; to exchange a symbolic experience; to learn or relearn something; to change a perception or cognition; to reduce uncertainty; to expand one's range of options; to exercise rational choices; to evaluate decisions; to control a process; to communicate an idea, a fact, or an opinion" (p. 22). Their typology of the primary information industries is shown in Table 3.2.

Not all information services and products reach the marketplace. Many of these are intermediate goods and services, produced in the process of manufacturing products and services for the primary information marketplace. A significant number of information services are produced by noninformation firms and information consumed internally. For example, the use of information obtained by remote sensing satellites is used in the fishing industry to locate schools and increase the catch. While not produced in an information industry, the information gathering by satellite is attributed to information consumed internally by the fishing industry. Another example is information activities performed in a firm that are consumed internally in order to produce the firm's products or services, for example, research and development, printing and publishing, photocopying, and so on.

Table 3.2 Typology of Primary Information Sector Industries

Knowledge Production and Inventive Industries
   R&D and Inventive Industries (private)
   Private Information Services

Information Distribution and Communication Industries
   Education
   Public Information Services
   Regulated Communication Media
   Unregulated Communication Media

Risk Management
   Insurance Industries (components)
   Finance Industries (components)
   Speculative Brokers

Search and Coordination Industries
   Search and Non-Speculative Brokerage Industries
   Advertising Industries
   Non-Market-Coordinating Institutions

Information Processing and Transmission Services
   Non-Electronic-Based Processing
   Electronic-Based Processing
   Telecommunication Infrastructures

Information Goods Industries
   Non-Electronic Consumption or Intermediate Goods
   Non-Electronic Investment Goods
   Electronic Consumption or Intermediate Goods
   Electronic Investment Goods

Selected Government Activities
   Primary Information Services in the Federal Government
   Postal Service
   State and Local Education

Support Facilities
   Information Structure Construction and Rental
   Office Furnishings

SOURCE: From *The Information Economy* (p. 23) by M. U. Porat and M. Rubin, 1977, Washington, DC: Government Printing Office.

Porat and Rubin referred to quasi-information activities, such as bureaucratic activities that have become commonplace in modern societies. Since the role of a bureaucracy is to ensure its continuity so that the rules of the organization will not change if the head of the organization is changed, it is essentially an information activity, producing,

Table 3.3 Partial Listing of Information Outputs that Constitute the Secondary Information Sector

---

Private Sector
  Printing and Publishing
  Telephone and Telegraph Communications
  Banking
  Credit Agencies
  Insurance Carriers and Brokers
  Real Estate Agents, Brokers, Managers
  Advertising Agencies

  Education
  Library Services
  Legal Services
  Data Processing

Government Sector
  Many of the above and in addition:
  Policy Planning
  Market Information Activities
  General Administration & Management
    Of the Civilian Bureaucracy
    Of the Military Bureaucracy

SOURCE: Adapted from *The Information Economy* (pp. 134-185) by M. U. Porat and M. Rubin, 1977, Washington, DC: Government Printing Office.

distributing, and consuming information. None of this information is sold in any marketplace but is consumed within the firm.

The federal government is an information industry, a public information industry with a multiplicity of information outputs paralleling those of the primary information sector, including, for example, printing and publishing, telecommunications, research and development, education, and more. There are also secondary information outputs, such as policy planning, market information activities, and the administration of the entire edifice. The federal information activities or industries shown in Table 3.3 are replicated, to a considerable extent, in state and local governments and are shown with examples of secondary information activities in private firms.

Almost all of the information activities that constitute the Primary Information Sector are essentially paralleled in the Secondary Information Sector, except that in the latter, the outputs do not reach the marketplace. However, in recent years, with increasing emphasis on reducing expenditures across all levels of government, many information activities that were formerly available only within government have been made available in the information marketplace: publications of reports, surveys, census data, research and development activities, legal services, and more. Additionally, private firms may decide to purchase, for example, accounting or data-processing services from established accounting and data-processing firms, rather than perform such services within their own firm. And such purchases would appear as the outputs of the Primary Information Sector, and the employees of these service suppliers would be counted among the information workers in the primary sector.

The Primary Information Sector, as defined by Porat and Rubin, is not too far removed from Machlup's definition of a knowledge industry. But as we noted, not all information activities take place in the marketplace, and the final product and service they produce are not always related to information. Besides the above differences, Machlup and Porat/Rubin also diverged on the information industry and information occupation relationship. Machlup insisted in keeping the two separate for fear of mixing with "information inputs in industries outside the information sector with outputs of industry in the information sector" (Machlup, 1962, p. 240).

Table 3.4 is a comparison of the Machlup, Bell, and Porat/Rubin definitions of information industries/activities as well as the categories adopted by the OECD in its analysis of the emerging information society.

Porat's and Machlup's analytical approaches were similar; both sought to define a set of occupations that were information- or knowledge-intensive, and with these analyses, define the information sector of the economy. They wished to account for the value added to the GNP by the information sector industries and to track the changing nature of work and workers. Porat used the National Income Accounts maintained by the Bureau of Economic Analysis in the U.S. Department of Commerce. These accounts assigned a code to every occupation in the nation, and he used these codes to define information tasks. The codes did not define the degree to which these occupations were information-intensive. The authors made judgmental decisions, often classifying certain tasks as 80% information work and 20% noninformation work. For example, they estimated that a physician's work would be 80% information work and 20% noninformation work, while a dentist's work would be 20% information work and 80% noninformation work.

Table 3.4 A Comparison of the Categories Used in Measuring Knowledge or Information Industries

Machlup	Bell	Porat & Rubin	OECD
Education	Higher education	Knowledge production & inventive industries	Knowledge producing
Research & development	R&D	Information distribution & communication industries	Search, coordination & risk management industries
Media of communication	Production of knowledge as intellectual property	Risk management	Information distribution & communication industry
Information machines		Search & coordination industries	Consumption & intermediate goods
Information services		Information processing & transmission services	Investment goods
		Information products industries	
		Selected government activities	
		Support facilities in information industries	

SOURCE: From *The Production and Distribution of Knowledge in the United States* (p. 361) by F. Machlup, 1962, Princeton, NJ: Princeton University Press; *The Coming of Post Industrial Society* (p. 213) by D. Bell, 1973, NY: Basic Books; *The Information Economy* (vol. 1, p. 50) by M. U. Porat & M. Rubin, 1977, Washington, DC: Government Printing Office; *Information Activities, Electronics and Telecommunication Technologies* (p. 18) by OECD, 1981, Paris: OECD.

Machlup restructured the National Income Accounts and did not split the information sector into two parts. Table 3.1 shows that while the two studies (Machlup and Government) were essentially identical in their broad categories, there were significant differences in the work activities defined. The Commerce study counted almost twice as many work groups as did Machlup.

More Recent Measurements of the Information Society

Following the early work of Machlup and Porat/Rubin, numerous studies were undertaken to further define the information society and the knowledge industries. Other countries sought to uncover their information societies and knowledge industries as well. Machlup's approach was used in a follow-up study of his original project, a study that he commissioned, managed, but failed to see through before his death in 1983 (Rubin & Huber, 1986). Porat and Rubin occupational categories were used in several other studies (Barnes & Lamberton, 1976; Lange & Rempp, 1977; Wall, 1977). In the early 1980s, the Organization for Economic Co-Operation and Development (OECD), recognizing the evolution of the information economies among its member nations, undertook to devise a comprehensive and systematic approach to monitor changes in employment, investment, consumer expenditure, trade flows, and market structure (OECD, 1981, p. 7). Rather than start afresh, OECD's Committee for Information, Computer and Communication Policy (ICCP) launched its investigation using Porat's list of occupation categories with but one change: collapsing market search and coordination specialists and information machine workers into one category, which they labeled information infrastructure occupations.

Through extensive work with national statistics, ICCP was able obtained data of 13 OECD member nations on the percentage, change, and components of the information workers, as well as each nation's percentage of information sector in GDP. From 1900 through 1980 the information sector steadily increased, while the agriculture and manufacturing sectors decreased. During this same period the services sector continued to increase, but with some variations. The largest percentage increase in the information work force in the major industrialized nations occurred between 1960 and 1970, 4.4% in the United States, 7.5% in Japan, almost 7% in Germany and Canada, with the United Kingdom and France increasing at about 4%. The rate of increase slowed down between 1970 and 1975; Japan continued to lead with an increase of 4.2%, followed by France at almost 4%, while the United States' information work force grew by about one-tenth of one percent, and little or no growth occurred in the United Kingdom. In general, in the industrialized nations the agricultural and industry work force continued to decline, except in Japan, where it grew, and both information and services work force continues to increase (see Table 3.5).

The OECD report was the first comparative study of its kind, but it reported only on the industrialized and highly developed nations in the West. Subsequent studies paid closer attention to the newly emerging or developing nations and industrialized nations in the Pacific Basin. Jussawalla, Lamberton and Karunaratne (1988, pp. 15-43) investigated both the primary and the secondary information sectors in seven Pacific countries: Fiji, New Zealand, Papua New Guinea, the Philippines, Malaysia, Singapore, and Thailand. Because of the significant differences one encounters in the definition of information work, cross-country comparisons are difficult to make, indeed are likely to yield a great deal of misinformation. We also question the degree of consistency in the maintenance of national statistics within a country. The information occupations as defined by the OECD often differ from definitions reported in data provided countries in their national reports. Consequently, a highly aggregated definition of the information sector consisting of the first four categories in the 1968 International Standard Classification of Occupations: Professional; Technical and Related Workers; Administrative, Executive, and Managerial Workers; and Clerical Workers is used. Similar aggregations for the other economic sectors were used by Katz in his studies. We use this approach in our determination of the contribution of the information sector to the productivity of the industry sector, a parameter in our definition of informatization, and we shall discuss the consequences of this approach in Chapter 6.

Katz (1986) examined work force structure in a number of developing nations, including Brazil, Egypt, India, South Korea, the Philippines, and Venezuela (pp. 209-228). We draw upon this work in Table 3.6 to illustrate the changes in the work force structure between 1960 and 1980.

All of these studies sought to measure just one set of parameters that determine informatization: size of the information sector work force relative to the other labor sectors. They all suffer from the same uncertainties we have previously identified: how differently the knowledge industries and the knowledge workers can be defined. There is

Table 3.5 Changes in the Work Force Among Four Industrialized Nations (in percent)

	1900	1910	1920	1930	1940	1950	1960	1970	1980
Information									
United States	12.8	14.9	17.7	24.5	24.9	30.8	42.0	46.4	46.6
United States*	14.8		18.5		25.2		42.0		48.0
United Kingdom	12.4	13.3	19.8	20.9	24.4	27.8	33.1	36.6	38.0
Germany						18.3	24.6	30.7	33.2
Australia		8.5	11.5	15.6	16.3	17.0	22.5	27.5	30.2
Services									
United States	25.1	17.7	17.8	19.8	22.5	19.0	17.2	21.9	28.8
United States*	25.0		19.0		21.7		18.5		28.8
United Kingdom	34.0	35.7	29.7	27.5	27.3	27.1	26.9	26.7	26.9
Germany						20.9			25.9
Australia		33.5	34.0	30.3	32.7	35.0	32.5	32.2	35.6
Industry									
United States	26.8	36.3	32.0	35.3	37.2	38.3	34.8	28.6	22.5
United States*	28.0		34.8		38.0		36.5		22.0
United Kingdom	45.4	43.4	43.2	45.2	42.6	39.9	36.1	33.7	31.5
Germany						38.3			35.1
Australia		27.0	27.5	30.9	32.0	33.0	33.0	31.2	26.7
Agriculture									
United States	35.3	31.1	32.5	20.4	15.4	11.9	6.0	3.1	2.1
United States*	37.5		34.5		16.0		5.0		2.2
United Kingdom	8.2	7.6	7.3	6.4	5.8	5.2	3.9	3.0	2.0
Germany						22.5			5.8
Australia		31.0	27.0	23.2	19.9	16.5	12.0	9.1	7.4

SOURCE: *The Information Economy: Development and Measurement (p. 121) by M. U. Porat and M. Rubin, 1977, Washington, DC: Government Printing Office. From "The Social Framework of the Information Society" by D. Bell, 1979, in M. Dertouzas and J. Moses (Eds.), The Computer Age: A Twenty-Year View, Cambridge: MIT Press; Four Sector Time Series of the U.K. Labour Force, 1841-1971 by S. D. Wall, 1977, London: U.K. Post Office, Long Range Studies Division; "The Theoretical Implications of Measuring the Communication Sector" by D. Lamberton, 1982, in M. Jussawalla and D. Lamberton, Communication Economics and Development, New York: Pergamon; Qualitative and Quantitative Aspects of the Information Sector by S. Lange & H. Rempp, 1977, Karlsruhe: Karlsruhe Institut dur Systemtechnik und Innovationsforschung.

Table 3.6 Changes in the Work Force Among Six Developing Nations (in percent)

	1960	1970	1980
Information			
Brazil	12.0	12.2	——
Egypt	8.0	12.4	18.6
India	4.4	6.6	7.6
S. Korea	6.3	10.1	14.6
Philippines	5.8	10.5	10.8
Venezuela	14.1	21.3	25.6
Services			
Brazil	16.2	24.5	——
Egypt	20.8	17.6	19.2
India	7.6	8.4	8.7
S. Korea	17.4	18.7	25.4
Philippines	14.6	19.4	22.0
Venezuela	30.4	31.9	34.9
Industry			
Brazil	15.9	17.4	——
Egypt	16.5	18.5	21.4
India	14.9	12.6	14.4
S. Korea	10.1	20.1	26.0
Philippines	13.5	15.2	15.2
Venezuela	21.4	23.5	25.0
Agriculture			
Brazil	55.8	46.0	——
Egypt	54.7	51.4	40.7
India	73.1	72.4	69.3
S. Korea	66.2	51.1	34.0
Philippines	66.1	54.9	52.1
Venezuela	34.1	23.4	14.5

SOURCE: Adapted from "Explaining Information Sector Growth in Developing Countries" by R. L. Katz, 1986, *Telecommunications Policy, 10*, pp. 209-228.

considerable evidence that the growth of the information sector, in comparison with the other sectors of the economy, is evidence of economic growth; generally, the larger the information sector, the higher the GNP/capita. There are several interesting anomalies indicating that size of a nation's information sector is not, by itself, a measure of its state of economic growth. For example, in 1987 Trinidad and West Germany both had information sectors of between 32% and 33% of the work force, but Trinidad's GNP per capita was about $5,000, while West Germany's was about $14,000. In that same year Panama and Australia had information sectors of between 28% and 30%, yet the GNP/capita of these countries were $2,000 and $10,000, respectively. The work information workers do contributes to the level of GNP, but simply having a large information sector may not be indicative of the degree to which informatization contributes to either the nation's wealth or the standard of living of its citizens. For example, with 18.6% of the working population considered to be in the information sector, the Egyptian industrial sector contributes about 35% to the nation's Gross Domestic Product; while in Algeria, the industrial sector contributes about 57% to that nation's GDP, with 21% of the working population in the information sector. Clearly, what these information workers do has a strong bearing on a nation's economy. In poverty-stricken Egypt, with high unemployment and heavy social welfare demands, a large number of workers classified as information workers are government employees providing health and welfare services. Indeed, government work is the job of last resort for the jobless. Industrial productivity has been necessarily sacrificed for public service.

Information Flow:
Words Transmitted and Words Consumed

Following the lead of Machlup, Bell, Porat, and the OECD, much of the research on the information economy has focused on attempts to define better ways of measuring the makeup and size of the information work force. Less work has been done to measure the diffusion of information and its flow, measures that are most meaningful for understanding progress toward an information economy. Machlup's success lies in the fact that he measured knowledge production and devised a measurable unit of analysis. He measured a diverse set of goods and services with a single, objective measure: value added in dollars. Information itself has many dimensions; economic, scientific, and behavioral. While Shannon has satisfied the engineer's need for a measure useful to the design of communications systems,[2] there have been few attempts to measure information and information flow in a manner that could lead to a better understanding of information consumption.

In 1969 the Japanese Information Study Group undertook to measure information flow (Ito, 1981, p. 680). "Information" in this study was not merely what is in print, but also any symbol, signal, or image having meaning to the parties at both the sending and the receiving ends. In addition, the information must be transmitted, with the sender's conscious will, to a receiver. Clearly, this required human intervention and excluded the programmed communications between computers without human participation. The Information Study Group faced the challenging task of developing a unit of analysis capable of being unambiguously measured. The "word" was selected as the unit of measurement, and an elaborate scheme was devised to allow for the conversion of speech, video, and even music into words in order to measure different forms of information. For example, a 1-minute color television broadcast translates into 1,320 words; but for a black-and-white broadcast, no more than 970 words were counted for the same time length. The content flow in face-to-face education was also included and, like color television, was assumed to have the highest rate of conversion to "words": 1,320 words per minute (Ito, 1981, p. 684). The Information Study Group developed measures to determine the quantity of information flow:

Information Supply: The amount of information transmitted by various sources through media, performance, or lectures. To adequately reflect the nature of mass media, the flow estimate was arrived at by multiplying the content of information in words by the size of the audience, for example, television sets in use.

Information Consumed: The amount of information consumed by the audience. For example, if a family watches an average of 3 hours of television per day, the amount of information consumed by viewing television will be 237,600 words (1,320 words/min × 180 minutes).

Information Cost: The cost of transmitting information, derived by subtracting the cost of information production from the total income of the information provider (and adding salaries of teachers for determining the information cost of education).

Distance of Information Flow: The total distance covered by the transmission of information. It is measured by "word-km" and is obtained by multiplying the amount of information consumed by the distance between senders and receivers. (Ito, 1981; Yoshizoe, 1986, pp. 58-82)

Only one similar project has been undertaken and that is in the United States by Ithiel de Sola Pool and his colleagues (Pool, Inose, Takasaki, & Hurwitz, 1984). Essentially the same approach utilized by the Information Study Group was adopted for the study on United States-Japan

Table 3.7 Annual Growth Rate in Per Capita Supply and Consumption of Information (in percent)

	Supply		Consumption	
	USA	Japan	USA	Japan
1960-1965	9.9	7.4	1.8	3.11
1965-1970	6.1	8.0	1.2	0.7
1970-1975	6.3	9.4	2.1	3.0
1975-1980	4.6	NA	1.5	NA

SOURCE: From *Communication Flows: A Census in the United States and Japan* (p. 42) by I. de S. Pool, H. Inose, N. Takasaki, & R. Hurwitz, 1984, Amsterdam: North-Holland. Copyright © 1984 by University of Tokyo Press. Reprinted by permission.

comparisons, with several adaptations to the differences in media and school structures in the two countries. These changes did not seriously jeopardize the comparability of the two studies. A comparison of these results is shown in Table 3.7.

The information flow census, like the measurements of the information sector and its work force, deals with one aspect of what has been described as an information society. The complexity of this approach to measuring information has probably limited its application to other countries.

Do These Measures Measure the Information Society?

We have reviewed the rich body of literature that has been compiled over the past three decades and more in order to explain and understand the emergence of the information society. It is a record of attempts to encompass, in a measurable fashion, the many facets of the information society. The reason for doing so is to enable one to chart the progress toward this society, primarily within a country. The definitional difficulties we have encountered make between-country comparisons difficult. We do not intend to compare nations as if they were in a footrace toward the goal of informatization, but rather to arrive at a means by which to determine how well a nation is progressing toward its own goal of informatization and development.

We have noted that a great deal of effort has been expended in determining the work force structure of a nation because, historically, as a nation industrializes, its information and service sectors increase while its agricultural sector decreases. It is not at all clear what is cause and what is effect. And, further, the paths toward an information society are often as varied as are the nations themselves.

Do these measures permit us to gauge a nation's progress toward informatization, toward the dual goals of economic growth and sociocultural development? Does the information obtained via these measures provide an adequate reflection of all the essential features of an information society? If not, what changes are required to do so?

The Problem of Value

Machlup was not unaware of the difficulties of measuring the knowledge industry. Often there were no physical outputs, productivity data, or a system for setting selling prices (Machlup, 1962, p. 44). Information was not similar to economic commodities; even when purchased, it was still available to other buyers. It is difficult to differentiate between knowledge and other goods: How do you set a value on knowledge in the form of research and development required to produce a computer or a chip, except in an aggregated fashion, and how do you allocate these knowledge costs below the industry level, that is, in the firm, department, or individual (Machlup, pp. 21-22, 47)?

Machlup acknowledged that knowledge measurement must take into account different types of knowledge. For example, there is "productive knowledge," which is expected to lead to increased productivity and a higher standard of living, and there is "unproductive knowledge," which may just serve to provide immediate pleasure. There is knowledge that may be offered free yet is not wanted, and there is knowledge that may cost a great deal to acquire. To *study* knowledge, an investigator must pay attention to these different hues because very often they are "joint products" (Machlup, p. 6). But in order to measure knowledge and information at all, such differences must be ignored.

Consequently, the U.S. Constitution would be measured in the same way as a 30-second television advertising spot. There is information acquired at a cost by Egyptian social workers that is used to achieve social goals but will not directly contribute to the GNP of the nation. However, this information will contribute to the quality of life of an individual and may make an individual healthy enough to be a productive worker and, thereby, indirectly contribute to the nation's GNP. Granted, it is impossible to directly determine from these measures if the life-style

Masuda envisioned for the information society is being achieved, for this would require measures of the quality of information being acquired. To equate knowledge or information production merely with the use of information machines, and label all workers employed in working with these machines as knowledge or information workers, leads to overestimation of the information work force. In doing so, university professors, talk show hosts, and bookbinders are assumed to be treated equally. While very few would argue that the production of books necessarily involves the binding process, and that even the most powerful supercomputers have to be packaged before shipment, the skills involved in accomplishing these jobs are essentially the same as those needed for many other types of labor that are not classed as knowledge or information work. Porat's decision to add a "support facilities" dimension to the information industry is especially troublesome to many observers. His model would claim that almost anyone involved in the production, transmission, and processing of information should be included in the measurement of an information industry. Since the production and distribution of information require that support facilities, buildings, furniture, office supplies, janitors and office cleaners, and the like are included in the measure of an information industry, should one therefore include the production and delivery of water, electricity, airconditioning, and other essential facilities in the workplace?

The danger of such inclusiveness is that one loses sight of the value of the work being performed. Information work is not necessarily high-value labor; data input jobs are among today's unskilled labor, and many jobs in such information industries as finance, insurance, real estate, and government are low-value jobs.

High-Value Information Work Creates Economic Growth

To effectively participate in the highly competitive global economy requires that the work performed be highly valued work, and it cannot be assumed that information work produces high-value products and services capable of finding a niche in the global marketplace. We have noted previously how a relatively large information work force in a nation may be primarily engaged in government public service, thereby adding only marginally, if at all, to the productivity required to compete in this global economy. A nation cannot achieve either economic growth or its goal of higher standards of living by becoming an information society, especially if the definition of such a society is the limited one of the percentage of workers engaged in information work. For example, in the United States, the world leader in the size of its information work force, the clearly defined information industries of finance, insurance, real estate, government and communications accounted for 27.6% of the Gross National Product in 1988. Agriculture, mining, construction, manufacturing, transportation, and public utilities (excluding communications) accounted for 40% of the GNP. The remaining 32.4% contribution to the GNP was provided by the service sector (U.S. Dept. of Commerce, 1991, p. 432).

The information sector has left considerable room for uncertainty regarding which activities, goods, and services are to be included and which are not. Consequently, when the definition of information goods is expanded to include all information machine manufacturing, the measures tend to overestimate the information sector, but when non-market-traded activities are excluded from the measure, it then tends to underestimate the sector size. Where to draw the line is a key issue in measurement validity.

Cross-National Comparisons Are Difficult

Comparisons between nations create additional measurement problems. For example, in most developed nations, medical workers must receive formal training and are expected to keep up with the most recent developments in the field. According to Porat's definition, education is part of the Primary Information Sector, and the medical profession is half-informational because activities such as subscription to professional magazines, accessing databases, and conducting tests and experiments contribute to the growth of an information industry. But in the Far East, where herbal medicine has been practiced for centuries and is still popular in many areas, "doctors" are also trained, but mostly through apprenticeships that traditionally involve not just learning how to diagnose and cure illness but also performing chores and errands for the master. The apprentice, by living with his teacher, is, in effect, part of the family. Once apprenticeship training is fulfilled, the apprentice will be practicing medicine based on what was learned during the apprenticeship, and its refinement through practice, but not much more than that. In this context, can the medical profession still be considered as information-related in, for example, China? The measurement of information flow, supply, and consumption has also been questioned, especially when attempts are made to perform cross-national comparisons. Of concern is the conversion ratio devised by researchers, in the United States and Japan, to transform visuals and music into words (Ito & Ogawa, 1984, p. 22; Yoshizoe, 1988, p. 54). It is difficult to understand the rationale that equates one minute of music to 120 words, and then to give the same number of words to one minute of color television and one minute of classroom lecture. Yoshizoe argues that the quantity of information transmitted by a medium should be determined by the unit cost of sending information by that medium. Yoshizoe's argument follows closely the mathematical theory of channel capacity (Shannon & Weaver, 1949). He compared his results with those obtained in the information flow studies and found wide differences that could only be explained by the inconsistencies of the conversion ratio (Yoshizoe, p. 81).

Pool and his colleagues recognized this difficulty and elected not to include the quantity of information transmitted by music and pictures in their study. The difference in the concept of "words" and how much information can be conveyed through each word in Japanese and in English continued to be nagging concern for the researchers and had to be explained away (Pool et al., 1984, p. 39).

The Johoka Index has not been subjected to the criticism encountered by the measures discussed above. One reason is that the statistical data required for that index are readily available, especially for the developing nations, from several sources, including government agencies and international organizations such as the ITU, UNESCO, and the OECD. The exception to this is the data required for determining the information ratio: the percentage of household expenditures on information. This ratio is calculated indirectly by subtracting noninformation expenditures (for food, clothing, energy, health care, etc.) from the total household expenditures, and it is assumed that what remains can be reasonably considered expenditures for information. This measure is clearly a Japanese-style measure, since it has been a custom for schoolchildren to obtain detailed household and family information on a day assigned by schools across the entire country, an activity that would meet with great resistance in the United States and other Western nations. Consequently, there is little evidence supporting its reliability and validity.

How to Use Measures Is the Critical Question

The quality of measures depends on how these measures are used and how findings are interpreted. We have noted the dangers of comparing information societies by information work forces, and Pool and his colleagues have raised doubts in the measuring of "words" in Japanese and in English. However, monitoring work force structure over time in a country provides valid indications of long-term trends within that country. Just what these trends portend is still up for discussion. Does the increase in the information sector necessarily lead to increases in GNP? Does the increase of information workers in the government sector necessarily mean little or no growth in GNP? There has been a clear transformation from agriculture to industry, and growth of both information and service sectors at the expense of the agricultural sector, and more recently the industry sector, have taken place over the past 150 years among the industrialized or developed nations. And the newly industrialized nations appear to be following similar paths. But there are important variations that must be explained if one wishes to use the work force measures effectively.

Infrastructure measures, such as the Johoka Index and the JIPDEC Index, are relatively easy to develop. With care they can be indicators of the degree of *access* to information a society has. Access to information and information technology is the necessary first step to their utilization and, in this respect, is a measure of the potential for social, political, and economic growth. However, there are numerous examples of heavy investments in the information and telecommunications technologies with little impact on GNP (e.g., Dordick, 1987).

In addition to its size, it is the quality of the work performed by the members of the information work force that contributes to a nation's economic growth and economic health. Consequently, we have added to the indices discussed a measure of the contribution of the information sector to the productivity of the manufacturing sector. In the next chapter we shall apply this and other measures to countries we have selected to represent three major categories of nations in order to determine if and how rapidly these countries are progressing toward informatization.

Notes

1. For a comprehensive discussion of this debate, see *Universal Telephone Service: Ready for the 21st Century* (1991), Annual Review of the Institute for Information Studies and, in particular, H. S. Dordick, "Toward a Universal Definition of Universal Services," pp. 109-139.

2. We refer to the concept of information as the reduction of uncertainty as formulated by Shannon and Weaver. See, for example, C. Shannon and W. Weaver (1949), *The Mathematical Theory of Communications*.

4

Informatization

Defining Informatization

Until recently the literature of the information economy has been primarily concerned with enumerating the number of information workers as a percentage of the nation's total work force.[1] The primary, indeed the traditional measure of the degree to which a society has moved toward being an information society was the size of the information work force. While this measure has been useful in indicating the informationalized nature of the society, it has been insufficient and often contradictory. As we noted in Chapter 3, there are nations in which the percentages of information workers are more or less identical, yet the gross domestic product (GDP, a measure of national wealth) and the GDP per capita (measure of the distribution of that wealth) are quite different.

In recent years several writers have expanded their view of information economies by including other indicators that provide a richer description of the level of informationalization of an economy. For example, Kuo (1989) has suggested infrastructure indicators such as mass media concentration, radio and television licenses, newspaper circulation, and telephone penetration.[2] Others have suggested the contribution of the information sector to the economy (Oniki & Kuriyama, 1989). We build on these descriptors for our definition of informatization. There are three dimensions to our definition of informatization: Infrastructure, Economic, and Social, drawing on the work of Kuo (1989).

Our Infrastructure Parameters are:
  Telephone main lines per 100 population
  Television sets per 1,000 population
  Newspaper circulation/1,000 population
  Amount of data terminal equipment on the public telephone and telex networks
Our Economic Parameters are:
  Percentage of information workers in the nation's work force
  Contribution of information sector to GNP/GDP
  Contribution of the information sector to productivity of the industrial sector
Our Social Parameters are:
  Rate of literacy
  Percentage of nation's school age population attending tertiary schools

Telephone Main Lines per 100 Inhabitants

Telephone density or penetration is a strong factor in economic growth. Hardy (1983) tested several hypotheses concerning the role of the telephone in economic development. We should note that these findings were given as preliminary and tentative ones, since the data on which they were based were quite limited. They should be viewed as hypotheses that require further testing but are, nevertheless, of value to our understanding of the importance of the telephone to national development.

1. Using Gross Domestic Product (GDP) or energy consumption (an often used measure of economic growth) as an indicator of economic development, the telephone facilitates economic development across all nations, both developed and developing.
2. With GDP/capita as an indicator of economic growth, economic growth facilitates telephone growth as it does energy per capita growth. This hypothesis, when added to the previous one, clearly indicates the difficulty in determining causation.

3. It is not clear that business telephone growth by itself facilitates economic growth. This would tend to support the notion that the public telephone network and the universal availability of telephone service to all segments of the population are, perhaps, more important for economic growth.

4. Economic development does facilitate residential telephone growth. Clearly, this follows from the availability of sufficient income for homeowners to obtain telephone service, in addition to telephone support programs such those available in the United States: Link-Up America and Life-Line.[3]

5. Interactive communications (the telephone) appears to have a greater influence on economic growth and development than the mass media.

6. It appears that the telephone does not make a greater contribution toward economic development for nations higher in the economic development scale than for nations lower on the scale, an important indicator of the importance of the telephone for development.

Recent research on the social uses of the telephone indicates that the effective use of the telephone, that is, the social uses of the telephone, is equally as important as its instrumental or purposeful uses (Dordick, 1989; Dordick & LaRose, 1992; Fischer, 1992). The telephone is frequently the preferred medium for the delivery of good and bad news, to chat and to relieve loneliness. The telephone is also the prime means for political polling, as well as for friends, family, and neighbors to discuss political issues prior to reaching decisions. That the telephone is important to the politics of a nation is evident by the care with which some nations ration its availability.[4]

We conclude that the telephone is a prime contributor to economic growth and social and political development.

Television Sets per 1,000 Inhabitants

We chose this measure of broadcasting rather than the number of broadcast stations in a country. Because the radio spectrum is a limited resource, there are, necessarily, relatively few broadcast stations available in any geographic area. Consequently, there may be few stations on the air. In countries where there were few broadcast outlets under government control, there are usually few television receivers. However, unless broadcast policies are established to ensure that diverse views are broadcast, even having a high percentage of households with television or radio would not guarantee the political pluralism that we often equate with political development. In democratic societies, such as the United Kingdom and France, ownership of few broadcast facilities was in the hands of the government in the past, and provisions were made to ensure, if not guarantee, that diverse views be heard. Citizen demands for a greater voice in their government and for increased access to news and information have been responsible, in part, for the end of the government broadcast monopoly in many nations. Further, modern technology has ended the era of spectrum scarcity; cable television and satellite-delivered broadcasting are increasing the number of voices and political views heard, and governments are having even greater difficulty maintaining their broadcast monopoly. As the number of broadcast and cable outlets increases, so does the number of television households. Consequently, we have elected to use this latter indicator.

Lerner and Schramm (1976; Schramm, 1964) stressed the importance of the mass media, and especially television, to raise the level of awareness of the developing peoples to the idea of the value in improving one's economic and social condition. Lerner suggested that television would develop empathy for modernization. Lerner also stressed the importance of television as a means to increase political participation, an important step toward political development.

Television does not require literacy. Therefore, in the early stages of a nation's development, it can communicate accepted national values and political attitudes. Therein lies a danger, for in nations in which the broadcast system is government-controlled, political development can be and has been stifled. On the other hand, some have claimed that national television can instill the idea of nationhood and the spread of a national language, as it has in Indonesia, to give but one example.

In a market economy, television, as well as radio and the print media, performs the important role of providing consumers with market information through advertising. While many observers of the mass media, and especially television, are highly critical of the extent to which advertisers control the media, nevertheless, advertising does play a significant role in a competitive marketplace by informing consumers of comparative prices and commodity choices.

Number of Newspapers per 1,000 Population

The number of newspapers per 1,000 population is often seen as a measure of political activity and democracy. However, it is more likely that the nature of newspaper ownership may be a more informed measure: The more diverse the ownership, the more likely there will be a diversity of views and a competition among political ideas.[5] However, this data is not readily available. Newspaper readership implies literacy and is, therefore, also a measure of social development. We cannot overlook the contribution newspapers make to a market economy through advertising and the development of informed consumers.

Amount of Data Terminal Equipment
on the Public Telephone and Telex Networks

This indicator broadly reflects the nation's level of informatization. It includes both personal terminals, such as personal computers, as well as data terminals in business and industry on telecommunications networks. Not only is this a measure of the nation's awareness of the importance and value of information, but it also reflects the importance of data communications, which could lead to integration of activities and higher levels of productivity that result from data and facilities sharing on a network. Data for this indicator have only recently become available and in only a relatively few nations. Nevertheless, we believe it is important to include this measure, for it may very well be the earliest manifestation of the importance of information in a society and, consequently, of the informatization of a society.

Policymakers have concentrated on communications infrastructures rather than information infrastructures. They have provided "transportation" rather than information and have sought to maximize access to this transportation system. New technology has increased the communicating capacity of the transport system, but it has not increased the ability of users to access the information being transported, except for voice communications on the public telecommunications network. While there are no barriers to the transmission of information, there are still barriers to its acquisition at the terminals of the network. In France public policy has resulted in more than 15,000 information services available to more than 30% of the households, through government-provided low-cost or free terminals on an intelligent network, thereby making it easy for households to access information.[6] In the United States, current policy has limited the extent to which intelligence on the network can reach the home, and a more expensive terminal, the personal computer, is required to access information.

Percentage of Information Workers
in the Nation's Work Force

Porat's early work established this measure of informatization. His comprehensive analysis of the U.S. work force required many assumptions concerning the nature of work, and approximations of the extent to which this work could be classed as information work. Similar approximations were made by other nations that performed similar analyses, often with wide variations in their definition of information workers. For example, in his enumeration of information workers in Japan, Kimeo Uno did not include secretarial workers and clerks, arguing that they did not originate information but merely processed other workers' information and should be counted as service workers (Uno, 1982).

In every industrialized nation and in many newly industrializing nations, the percentage of information workers in the society has been increasing, while the numbers of agricultural and industry workers has been decreasing. As we reviewed in our first chapter, many scholars have stated that this is the primary evidence of the shift toward an information era.

The information sector offers exceptional opportunities for economic growth, not only from its own output but also from the productivity it stimulates in other sectors. Further, the information products and services are high valued ones and could command higher returns on investments.

The information sector requires an educated and highly skilled work force and a high level of literacy. The shift toward an information economy is in response to the globalization of the economy and the interdependency created by world trade. Such an economy requires a modern telecommunications infrastructure. A large information sector should contribute significantly to a nation's Gross Domestic Product (GNP/GDP) and to raising the standard of living of its citizens.[7]

The size and nature of the information sector is the key measure in defining an information society. For in the final analysis, it is what people do that defines their culture and their society.

Contribution of the Information Sector
to the Gross Domestic Product

Students of information economics argue that in advanced industrial economies, the information sector is a dominant one, having taken over from the manufacturing sector. They further suggest that it is a strong contributor to the nation's Gross Domestic Product. In newly industrializing and developing nations, employment in the information sector is small, but growing faster than employment in other sectors of the economy. In Singapore and Taiwan the information sector work forces are growing rapidly, but are still smaller than employment in the manufacturing and service sectors. In the highly industrialized nations, such as the United States and in Europe, information sector employment has been level for several years, while employment in the manufacturing sector continues to decline and employment in the service sector is now growing.

What is important to our analysis is not merely the size of the information sector, but also its contribution to the nation's standard of living, to its gross national or domestic product. For example, the information sectors in Egypt and Israel are about the same. However, the contribution of the Egyptian information sector to that nation's GNP is much less than the sector's contribution to GNP in Israel. The reason for this is that a large number of the Egyptian information workers are providing government social services for a society that is largely poor, unemployed, and in need of social services, while many of the information workers in Israel are engaged in relatively high-value manufacturing and service tasks as well as research and development.

This indicator has been extensively explored by Jussawalla and others, albeit not in all of the nations we shall be examining (see, e.g., Jussawalla, Lamberton, & Karunaratne, 1988). In our work, we do not intend to perform the complex econometric analysis required to determine the contribution of the information sector to a nation's GDP, and will draw upon the referenced works.

Contribution of the Information Sector to the Productivity of the Manufacturing Sector

How much the information sector contributes to the GDP depends on the contribution of the information sector to the productivity of the economy. Contrary to expectations, the expansion of the information sector has not always been followed by increases in a nation's productivity. Indeed, those industries that have invested heavily in information technology, such as the finance and banking and merchandising sectors, often have not shown the expected increases in productivity (Dordick, 1987). The reasons for this are several. The introduction of information technology requires extensive worker training and debugging of the equipment and software, which takes considerable time. Another reason is that productivity gains are distributed across the firm, at different times, thereby delaying significant productivity gains. Attempts to quantify the contribution of the information sector to the productivity of the manufacturing sector have been marginally successful (see, e.g., Oniki & Kuriyama, 1989). Analyzing specific sectors is the preferred way to attack this question; however, that would be beyond the scope of this book. We shall use a method that enables us to examine the contribution of the information sector to the manufacturing sector of an economy, using aggregate data derived from existing sources.

Rate of Literacy and Percentage of Nation's School-Age Population Attending Tertiary Schools

Information has always been "a useful thing" (*Webster's*, 1966), which can be bought and sold in newspapers, on radio and television, from bankers and stock brokers, and in libraries, where information is available to all and paid for by the taxpayers. Information has a variable value, depending on its timeliness and its source, and there are both individuals who charge considerable sums for the timely information they provide and individuals who are willing to pay considerable sums for that information. Fortunes have been made by having the right information at the right time. For example, the news of Napoleon's defeat at Waterloo, delivered by carrier pigeon to the Rothschilds, is reported to have set that family on its road to immense wealth.

However, to most people, the usefulness and value of information may not be as readily apparent as that of other consumer goods. Undoubtedly there are many who would question the value of information as a good because it cannot feed, or clothe, or improve material life. It is not surprising, then, that the mass media, perhaps our most important form of information, is seen by many primarily as entertainment, by some as information and news, and by a smaller number as education.

Information is a product of great value, not only for economic reasons but also for achieving the quality of social, cultural, and political life that developing countries strive for. Knowing how to acquire and effectively use information leads to knowledge of the value and importance in achieving these objectives. No nation can expect to compete in a global economy in which information has become an important, high-value product without a skilled work force and a literate population. Not only will this population contribute to economic growth but it will also significantly impact the political and social development of the nation.

In an information age, information in all its forms will proliferate. Although traditional literacy, that is, reading and writing, may not be necessary to appreciate video and audio information, it is absolutely necessary for other forms of information. But literacy by itself is not sufficient. Education creates the awareness of the world around people that enhances the value of information to them. Training to learn how best to use the growing number of information technologies that make access to information possible is absolutely necessary. Consequently, tertiary education is an equally important prerequisite for informatization. The percentage of the population, either with tertiary education or enrolled in institutions providing tertiary education, is not only an indication of the quality of the labor force but also of how skilled the populace is in utilizing education.

Notes

1. See, among far too many to be referenced here, Barnes and Lamberton (1976), Jussawalla and Lamberton (1982), Porat (1977), Katz (1988).

2. See Kuo (1989), also the JIPEC and RITE measures discussed in Chapter 3.

3. See Dordick and Fife (1991) for a discussion of telephone assistance programs in the United States and their impact on telephone penetration.

4. During the early years, for example, Israel rationed the telephone so that the military and government officials received access before the general public. Similar restrictions have been in place for years in the former Soviet Union and in China.

5. For example, Ben Bagdikian (1983) has a very strong case in favor of ownership diversity and against newspaper chains arguing that diversity of ownership supports political pluralism.

6. We refer to the Teletel infrastructure and the Minitel terminals that are available to telephone subscribers in France.

7. In the analyses that follow we use Gross Domestic Product (GDP)—the total final output of goods and services produced by the country's economy, that is, within the country's territory by residents and nonresidents.

5

Looking for the Infrastructure:
Charting the Measures

How far we have come on our way toward the information society? As we discussed in Chapter 2, the concept of the information society is by no means unidimensional. To tackle this question, we examine advances towards informatization, according to the three parameters outlined in Chapter 4. In this chapter we examine the availability of infrastructure; in Chapter 6, the progress made in achieving economic goals; and in Chapter 7, progress in achieving the social goals of informatization.

The Information Infrastructure

A necessary condition for achieving a high degree of informatization is access to information and to information technology. The efficient production, distribution, and consumption of information require an information infrastructure utilized by an educated and trained work force. With data from major international organizations, including UNESCO, International Telecommunications Union, and World Bank, we examine this infrastructure, its distribution throughout the world, its growth rate, and its contribution to informatization.

Mass media is the primary means for the wide distribution of information, and the telephone performs that function for point-to-point distribution of information. Increasingly, the computer and other data terminals have become important for the transport of data for managing, coordinating, and controlling business operations and for performing many transactions in a citizen's daily life. Adequate data for examining the significance of information and telecommunications infrastructure to informatization is available for the telephone and, to a limited extent, data terminals on telecommunications networks, and for the major mass media: newspapers, radio, and television.

The World Bank utilizes per capita GDP as a way to distinguish four groups of nations: low-income economies, lower-middle-income economies, upper-middle-income economies and high-income economies. To facilitate cross-group comparisons, we adapt the 1989 World Bank approach, but with the lower-middle- and upper-middle-income economies combined into middle-income nations (See Appendix B, Table 1).[1]

We are also interested in country differences, for in this way we can obtain a better understanding of specific factors that affect economic growth. Recognizing that adequate data is not available for all of the countries within these categories, we have selected the 19 shown in Appendix B, Table 2, to assist us in the analyses that follow. Where possible we shall discuss cross-group comparisons, using the World Bank's categories; otherwise, we shall use the abbreviated version. We have found this approach useful to understanding the changing nature of worldwide informatization.

Telephone Main Lines

The world telecommunications equipment market grew by more than 50% between 1986 and 1990, from $81 billion to $125 billion. This is a growth rate of about 10% per year. In 1990, 36% of sales were to North America, 47% to Europe, 13% to Asia, and just under 3% to Latin America and Africa. As one might expect, the most rapid growth rate was in Africa, where telecommunications is least developed, and the slowest rate was in North America, which is most highly developed (Table 5.1).

Table 5.1 World Telecommunications Market Growth by Region (1985-1990)

Region	Growth Rate (%)
North America	3.0
Europe	4.6
Asia	6.2
Latin America	6.1
Oceania	4.9
Africa	7.7

SOURCE: From *NTIA Telecom 2000* (p. 328), Washington, DC: US Department of Commerce, 1991.

Despite the liberalization of telecommunications markets in many nations, market entry for competitive providers remains difficult, especially in those countries where there is a state-owned and -operated telecommunications provider. Reviewing various OECD as well as industry reports over the years has shown that no more than seven corporations usually accounted for more than 70% of the telecommunications market in each of the nations under study. The manufacture of telecommunications equipment, including the large computer-controlled switches that manage the network, are in the hands of relatively few providers, with almost 42% of the 1986 sales by corporations in the United States (Table 5.2). These same firms are also the major providers of customer premises equipment as well as other systems, often including cable and fiber. We find that 60% of the digital lines were placed in service in 1985 by three firms (Table 5.3). Almost 90% the telecommunications equipment sold in 1989 was provided by 27 companies, of which 9 were in the United States, 13 in Western Europe, and five in Japan (United Nations, 1989; United Nations Industrial Development Organization, 1989).

The development of a nationwide public switched telephone network (PSTN), the backbone of a nation's telecommunications infrastructure, is very capital-intensive. Major investments are required before revenue can be created. Further, efficiently operating and maintaining a PSTN requires trained engineers and other staff, and in many countries these resources are not available. The highly concentrated telecommunications industry prefers to market in nations that are well along the way toward the construction of their infrastructure, to ensure rapid payment and avoid risks that might arise in politically unstable states.

Table 5.2 World's Top Ten Telecommunications Equipment Manufacturers

Company	Headquarters	1986 Sales ($ billions)
AT&T	United States	10.2
Alcatel	Belgium	8.0
Siemans	Germany	5.4
NEC	Japan	4.5
Northern Telecom	Canada	4.4
IBM	United States	3.3
Motorola	United States	3.1
Ericsson	Sweden	3.1
Fujitsu	Japan	2.1
Philips	Netherlands	2.8

SOURCE: From *NTIA Telecom 2000* (p. 329), Washington, DC: US Department of Commerce, 1991.

According to the International Telecommunications Union, average telephone penetration of all reporting nations grew by 187% from 1970 to 1980 and by about 75% during the last decade of the 1980s. However, telephone density is highly skewed. In the high-income nations telephone main lines per 1,000 inhabitants ranged from 506 in the United States to 356 in Singapore in 1989, with an average of about one telephone per family. In that same year telephone main lines in middle-income nations averaged 80 lines per 1,000 inhabitants, ranging from 378 main lines per 1,000 inhabitants in Greece to 18 per 1,000 inhabitants

Table 5.3 Digital Lines Placed in Service Worldwide in 1985 (in percent)

	Lines
Northern Telecom (Canada)	25
AT&T (United States)	21
Alcatel (France)	14
GTE (United States)	8
Ericsson (Sweden)	8
NEC (Japan)	8
Siemans (West Germany)	6
ITT (United States)	4
Other	6

SOURCE: From *NTIA Telecom 2000* (p. 315), Washington, DC: US Department of Commerce, 1991.

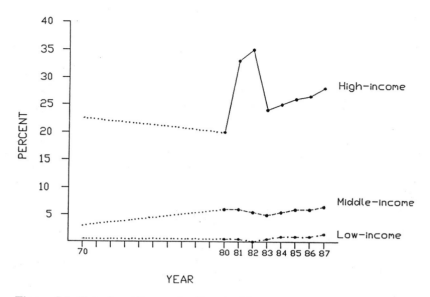

YEAR

Figure 5.1. Telephone Penetration Rate by Three Nation Groups

SOURCE: *Yearbook of Common Carrier Telecommunication Statistics,* Geneva, Switzerland: ITU, various years; *UNESCO Statistical Yearbook,* Paris: UNESCO, various years.

in Guatemala. Among the low-income nations, the figure varied from a low of one phone per 1,000 inhabitants in Burundi, Mali, and Rwanda to a high of 18 per 1,000 in Burma, or an average of about 4 phones per 1,000 inhabitants. After the worldwide economic recession of 1983-1984, telephone penetration among the high-income nations grew rapidly. This growth was not paralleled among the middle- and low-income nations, and consequently, the gap between the high-income nations and the middle- and low-income nations widened (Figure 5.1).

When individual nations are compared, disparities are even more pronounced. In 1981 telephone density in the United States was 115 times greater than the average among African countries, 46 times more than that in Asia, and almost 17 times greater than in Latin America (Johnstone & Sasson, 1986). Seventy percent of the world population is in Third World nations, but they have barely 7% of the world's telephones (Elkington & Shopley, 1985, p. 5). These ratios have not changed significantly in the years since 1981. Further, compare the average telephone main lines (per 100 inhabitants) among the high-income nations with those among the low-income nations given in Table 3 in Appendix B. We find a ratio of about 40 to 1 in 1986, while the ratio of high-income nations to middle-income nations is about 3 to 1. There are wide differences in telephone main lines/100 population rates within a country group. This is especially so among the middle- and low-income groups; in both cases, the difference between the lowest and highest penetration is greater than 75%. This reflects the very uneven growth in telephone infrastructure investments in many of these nations still struggling to provide for the basic needs of their people.

There are also wide disparities between urban and rural areas in many countries; for example, up to 30,000 communities are inaccessible by telephone in Mexico, and even in the United States there are rural areas in several southern states in which telephone service is not yet available (Dordick & Fife, 1991). The decline of the Soviet Union and its Eastern European allies ushered in the need for modern telecommunications infrastructures in order to attract foreign capital, and this has led to several joint ventures between U.S. firms and national Postal Telephone and Telecommunications organizations. This will certainly lead to more rapid diffusion of telephones in many middle-income nations.[2] Many of these ventures are geared to the construction of systems to serve primarily business and industry and are not likely to lead to the development of a PSTN. In any case the gap between the middle- and high-income nations is likely to decrease, resulting in a widening gap between the middle-income and low-income nations, an outcome that will add to their inability to informatize and compete in the global economy.

Computers and Other Data Terminals

No society can exist without information; information is necessary in all aspects of daily life and certainly for performing transactions of all kinds. There are many historians who argue that information societies have been with us since the dawn of history.

More than a decade ago, many newly industrialized as well as developing nations saw semiconductor manufacturing as their entrée into the information industry and core technologies identified with the information society. They welcomed the location of firms from the more highly developed nations. Even a casual examination of the innards of Apple, IBM, and other personal computers reveal suppliers in Malaysia,

Indonesia, Mexico, Thailand, and other nations. Information systems—mainframes and microcomputers, terminals and telecommunications equipment—is a volatile sector, frequently bombarded by rapid technological innovation resulting in rapid obsolescence. Semiconductor manufacturing is a very cyclical business, reflecting the demand for computers and other information technologies. The United Nations Industrial Development Report reported that in 1984 worldwide semiconductor production grew by 46%, to reach $32.75 billion in value. Just one year later, production fell by 12%, although growth was renewed, reaching a new peak of 30% in 1988, only to be followed by a decline in production in the early 1990s (United Nations, 1990).

Information technology investments require not only considerable capital but also special skills and frequently result in the restructuring of the management of the adopting firms. There are also relatively long learning curves following often painful periods of software debugging, resulting in uncomfortably long periods of low productivity. It is not surprising that the computer industry is greatly influenced by economic cycles (see, e.g., Morgan & Sayer, 1988). In 1990 information systems revenue of the world's major suppliers grew by about 9%, considerably less than 1987 and 1988 figures, but already up from the 1989 crash rate of 5% (Kelley, 1991). The recovery, however, was neither strong enough nor long enough to offset a wave of layoffs, termination of marginal product lines, and industry mergers leading to further downsizing. In 1992 industry revenue grew at 6%, pushing manufacturers to turn to software and services for profit (Verity, 1992).

Just as large telecommunications network switches and construction is a highly concentrated industry, so is the world's mainframe industry, with relatively few companies in few nations that are market leaders. Eight of the 10 largest companies have been unchallenged leaders since 1987 (Kelley, 1991). Of the 10, IBM was the largest, a multinational kingdom in itself. In 1989 IBM alone accounted for nearly one-fourth of the revenue of the world's top 100 suppliers. Not only did it account for a large share of the revenues, it was also the market leader in every country, except the former Soviet Union and its satellites and Japan, and was 8 to 10 times the size of its nearest rivals (Morgan & Sayer, 1988, p. 81).

The manufacture of microcomputers and data terminals and other equipment required for information systems is widely distributed among many small firms in the highly industrialized nations in the world. IBM clones assembled in Malaysia, Taiwan, Singapore, the Republic of

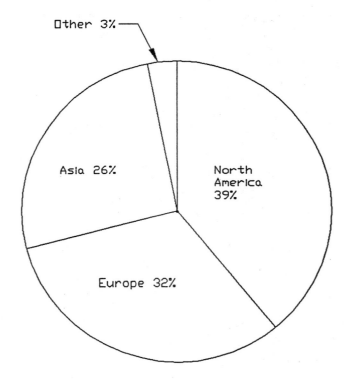

Figure 5.2. World Distribution of IT Trade

SOURCE: Kelly, J., "Information Technology Sales Soar to $256B," *Datamation,* June 15, 1991, p. 27. Reprinted by permission of Cahner's Publishing Company.

Korea, and Hong Kong once flooded the market, and IBM and Apple compatibles are big business in the United States. Nevertheless, the world leaders are in North America, Japan, and Western Europe. There are significant regional imbalances in the diffusion of information technology.

North America leads in information technology trade, followed by Europe and Asia (primarily Japan), as shown in Figure 5.2. In 1987 it was estimated that more than half of the computers in use were found in the United States, with Europe accounting for 22%, and Japan for 11%. Other countries (Taiwan, Korea, and the former USSR) accounted for 16% of the world's computers. In terms of computer power (measured in MIPS) the U.S. share is further heightened, as shown in Figure 5.3. The United

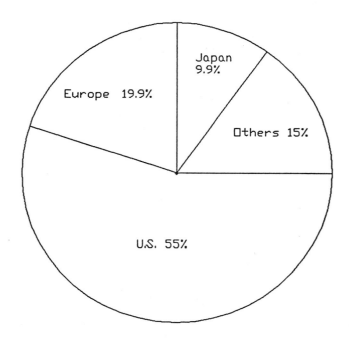

Figure 5.3. World Distribution of Computer Power in MIPS

NOTE: The figures are from year end 1987.
SOURCE: From Egil Juliussen and Karen Juliussen, *The Computer Industry Almanac,* Incline Village,
NV: Brady, 1988.

States could boast of more computer power than all other nations combined (Juliassen & Juliassen, 1989, pp. 5-25).

The concentration of computer facilities affects the development of software and database industries, so necessary for an information economy. The U.S. share of the world software market in 1987 was 52%, followed by Japan, which had 44% of that market. In 1987 the United States still accounted for more than 50% of the more than 1,000 databases available worldwide (with almost 200 million records).

As important as the computer is in the information age, to date no international organization has been charged with the task of systematically collecting data on computer penetration rates on a global level. The available data is far from complete, as can be seen by the following information we have for the years 1986-1987, from which information from most of the developing nations are missing worldwide.

Table 5.4 Computer Penetration (per 1,000 population)

	1986	1987
World	14	16
United States		167
India	< 3 per 10,000 population	
People's Republic of China	< 3 per 10,000 population	
Brazil	3 per 10,000 population	
Mexico	3 per 10,000 population	
Republic of Korea	9	12
Singapore		65

SOURCE: Adapted from *The Computer Industry Almanac* by E. Juliussen and K. Juliussen, 1988, Incline Village, NV: Brady.

Worldwide average computer penetration rates were 14 and 16 per 1,000 inhabitants in 1986 and 1987, respectively, approximately 9% of the U.S. figure, as shown in Table 5.4. Penetration was low in most of the developing nations; in both India and China, for example, there were fewer than 3 computers per 10,000 inhabitants in 1987. Computer penetration in the newly industrialized nations was also low, 3 per 1,000 persons in Brazil and Mexico. Taiwan reported 9 computers per 1,000 inhabitants in 1986 and 11 per 1,000 inhabitants in 1987. South Korea reported 9 per 1,000 inhabitants in 1986 and 12 per 1,000 inhabitants in 1987. Singapore, heavily engaged in entrepot activities for which data processing is a necessity, reported computer penetrations of between 35% and 38% of penetration in the United States.

Even among the more developed nations differences in computer penetrations are substantial. The U.S. rate, for example, is more than three times that of Australia and of Western Europe. Indeed, the U.S. rate is 1.7 times that of the United Kingdom, the leader in Europe. Data are missing from most socialist nations, but in the former Soviet Union computer penetration rate was estimated to be at 1 per 1,000 inhabitants in 1987.

While the total number of computers in a nation, stand-alone as well as networked, do indicate a level of informatization, networking for data communications indicates a degree of informatization that leads more directly to the purpose of information technology, that is, increasing productivity. World Development Reports provide information on networked data terminal equipment using the PSTN or telex networks.

However, liberalization in the United States and other nations has resulted in many private networks that interconnect firms across the nation and, indeed, the world. Data terminal equipment on these networks is not reported on Table 6 in Appendix B. For example, a major percentage of networked data terminal equipment in the United States is on private networks, as is that in Japan and Singapore. On the other hand, West Germany, France, and the United Kingdom (prior to 1984) did not permit private networks. Consequently, the data provided in Appendix B, Table 4, accurately reflect the growth in data communications in these nations. Most developing nations have not liberalized their telecommunications, and the information in Appendix B, Table 4, do reflect the growth of their data communications capability. Among those industrialized nations that restrict data communications over PSTN or telex networks, the average increase in data communications between 1980 and 1987 was about 160%. The very sparse data for developing nations do not permit any estimate of average growth rates, but growth records in individual nations are noteworthy. Malaysia, for example, has increased its data communications by almost 500% during the period of 1984 to 1986. Between 1983 and 1987 Thailand also experienced a more than 500% increase, and Zimbabwe about a 50% increase in its data communications. One exception was the Philippines, where a decrease of about 17% in data communication was observed during this same period. Data communications are considered important for achieving informatization with all nation groups experiencing significant growth. The middle- and low-income countries engaged in semiconductor and microprocessor assembly or manufacture for multinational corporations exhibited rapid growth in data communications. The decline of data communications capability in 1983 through 1985 in the Philippines can probably be attributed to the severe political difficulties in that nation, resulting in the reduction of manufacturing activity by multinationals that had been operating in that country, and by the loss of a good portion of the educated work force for job opportunities and political security elsewhere.

The Mass Media:
Radio, Television, and Newspapers

Differences in the mass media penetration rates among countries are less dramatic when compared with the telecommunications, computers, and other data terminal equipment. Nevertheless, the uneven distribution and resource disparities continue to concern researchers today, as they did Schramm and the economic planners in 1964.[3] In the decade of the 1970s, world radio penetration increased from about 21 to 55 receivers per 1,000 population, and television from just about 3 to 10 sets per 1,000 inhabitants. Newspaper circulation also increased during the period but failed to keep up with population growth, going from 15 newspapers per 1,000 inhabitants to 16 per 1,000 (Stevenson, 1988, p. 100).

The growth, however, did not significantly offset the disparity between the more-developed and the less-developed nations. By the end of the '70s the Third World had 71% of the world's population but only 15% of the radio receivers and 17% of the television sets. Yearly newsprint consumption in the developing world averaged less than one kilogram per person, in contrast to about 18 kilograms per person in the industrialized nations. There were also disparities among Third World nations: The majority of the mass media were found in Latin America, with much of Africa and Asia remaining outside media reach (Stevenson, 1988, p. 102).

During the 1980s two encouraging trends in the worldwide distribution of electronic mass media emerged. While the growth of both radio and television significantly slowed in the industrialized nations, growth continued at a significantly greater rate in the Third World nations. According to a BBC estimate, the Third World share of radio increased from 15% to 19% from 1970 to 1980, and its share of television receivers from 8% to 13%.

Beginning in the mid-1980s all nation groups showed a rather steady growth in the penetration of television receivers into the home (see Figure 5.4). Between 1980 and 1989 the high-income nations increased their share of the world's television sets per 1,000 inhabitants by a modest 29%, a reflection of the high level of penetration already achieved. Indeed, in some of these nations household penetration of television sets had reached 98%, often greater than telephone penetration. Among the middle-income nations the increase in the decade was about 305%, and among the low-income nations the increase in the decade was 361%. In 1970 low-income nations had, on average, less than 8 television receivers per 1,000 persons. At the end of 1980 they reported an increase of 448%.[4] In the 1980s the growth rate was considerably slower.

In 1989 television receiver penetration in the high-income nations was more than three times greater than in the middle-income nations, and 25 times greater than in the low-income nations.

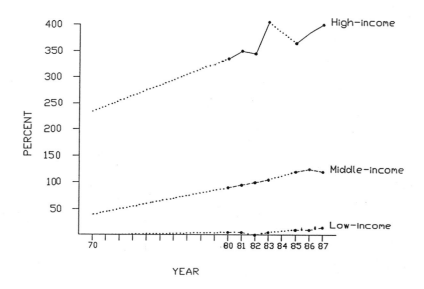

Figure 5.4. Television Penetration Rate by Three Nation Groups
SOURCE: *UNESCO Statistical Yearbook*, Paris: UNESCO, various years.

Turning to specific country differences, given in Appendix B, Table 4, note that the television sets per 100 tend to be highest in those nations in which there are multiple broadcasters. Furthermore, in those nations showing a strong increase in television set penetration, essentially all but Germany, Singapore, and New Zealand, there appears to be the availability of a mix of commercial and public or government broadcasters. However, both Germany and Singapore can receive programs from neighboring nations, either over the air or by cable; consequently, in recent years there has been a rapid increase in television set penetration.

Among the middle-income nations, all nations have had either a mix of commercial and government broadcasters or commercial only, hence the steady growth in television set penetration. The record is clear among the low-income nations; Egypt, Thailand and the Philippines have several commercial broadcast stations, while India and Indonesia depend entirely upon government broadcasting.

Radio, the most important mass medium in distributing development messages to policymakers and development planners in the 1960s and

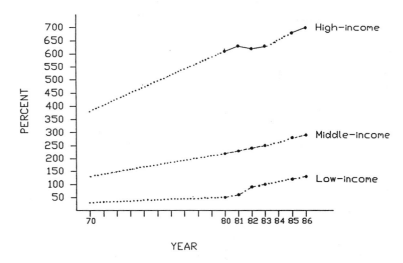

Figure 5.5. Radio Penetration Rate by Three Nation Groups
SOURCE: *UNESCO Statistical Yearbook,* Paris: UNESCO, various years.

1970s, remains the most popular medium of all. In the highest-income nations almost every family has an average of two radio receivers (see Figure 5.5), and the middle-income group has one set per family.

Because of the requirement for literacy, newspapers have always been seen as an urban medium, and for upper-income people. Scarcity of data makes it difficult to obtain an accurate global picture of newspaper availability. With limited data, we estimate that in 1970 the average global newspaper penetration was about 136 per 1,000 inhabitants. Eighteen years later newspaper penetration increased by 9%, to about 148 newspapers per 1,000 inhabitants. The average penetration of newspapers per 1,000 in the high-income nations in 1988 is 315; for middle-income nations, 96; and low-income nations, about 17 newspapers per 1,000 inhabitants.

There is a tendency for higher personal income nations and higher literacy nations to have higher newspaper penetration. But with the growth of television in the high-income nations, newspaper penetration fell from about 373 newspapers per 1,000 inhabitants in 1980 to 315 newspapers per 1,000 inhabitants in 1988. This has also occurred in low-income nations; as television penetration increased, newspaper

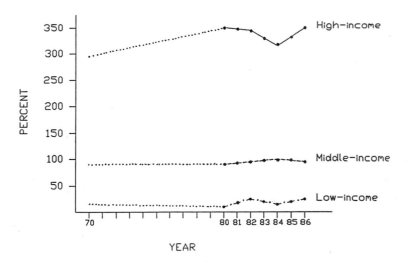

Figure 5.6. Newspaper Penetration Rate by Three Nation Groups
SOURCE: *UNESCO Statistical Yearbook,* Paris: UNESCO, various years.

penetration remained at around 17% in 1988, about the same as the 1970 average rate (Figure 5.6).

But there are vast differences among the nations, ranging among the high-income nations from 566 newspapers per 1,000 inhabitants in Japan, to 225 in Canada in 1986 (see Appendix B, Table 5). Among the middle-income nations, where data is scarce, Malaysia reported 323 newspapers per 1,000, while Brazil reported 57 per 1,000. Among the low-income nations, the range is much narrower, with about 50 newspapers per 1,000 in Egypt, and only 16 per 1,000 in Indonesia for 1986.[5]

We must be cautious in drawing conclusions from this data. Nations in the low- and middle-income groups do not often have credible newspaper auditing systems, and the number of reporting agencies tallying and providing newspaper circulation information is much smaller than for other information media. However, the declining trend in newspaper penetration is so consistent that we cannot dismiss the findings as purely coincidental.

We often overlook the mass media in discussions of the information society. We must keep in mind that the mass media play an important role in the informatization process as a facilitator of political development as well as the marketplace.

Not to be overlooked are the new media that have entered the marketplace since the early 1980s. The videocassette recorder (VCR) is found in all nations—high-, medium-, and low-income nations—often to the discomfort of national planners.

Unlike radio and television, which reached 30% penetration in the United States in about 5 years, the VCR required about 11 years to reach that penetration in 1985. In the 6 years since then, the VCR is estimated to have reached 80% of U.S. households. Worldwide it is estimated that in 1991 the VCR can be found in one-third of all TV households ("World VCR," 1991). The VCR has infiltrated nations with the most hostile regulations and guarded markets. The penetration rate of the VCR was rising rapidly in Bangladesh and Taiwan, despite government bans on importing VCRs. In Taiwan smuggling VCRs had become so lucrative that the government lifted the ban (Wang, 1986). In many corners of the socialist and Islamic world, audiences quietly entertained themselves with video material banned from broadcasts and motion picture houses.

In nations where media content is highly regulated, audiences found videocassette recorders a new venue for video entertainment. Islamic, oil-exporting nations are among those with the highest rates of VCR penetration in TV households in 1988: Kuwait (78%), Bahrain (63%), United Arab Emirates (75.9%), Saudi Arabia (51.7%), and Qatar (68.7%) (UNESCO, 1989). Some of the poorest nations also had a substantial percentage of the television households equipped with VCRs, among them are India (49.3%), Sri Lanka (33.8%), Zimbabwe (30.7%), and a score of African nations (Klee, 1991). It is safe to say that today the diffusion of VCRs is proceeding very rapidly throughout much of the world, often by as much as 25% per year. Clearly, in nations with very limited broadcast diversity, the VCR is extremely popular and in great demand. There is a very high correlation between video piracy and the lack of video diversity (Ogan, 1989) (Figure 5.7).

Some Conclusions

Machlup, Masuda, Porat, and Bell argued that information- and knowledge-based activities will become the driving forces in future societies. In all nations, both industrialized and industrializing, among low-, middle-, and high-income nations, the information infrastructure is growing. The data reviewed are indicative of aggregate trends rather than absolute measures. In comparing the penetration of information media among nations, there are very interesting patterns of development.

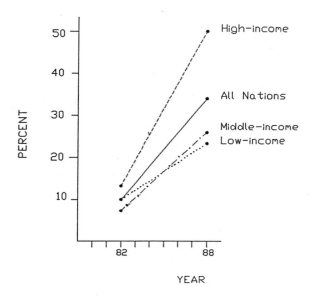

YEAR

Figure 5.7. VCR Penetration Rate by Three Nation Groups (per 100 TV Families)

SOURCE: *World Communication Report,* Paris: UNESCO, 1989, and from "Video Cassettes—Past, Present, and Future" by B. Fox, 1983. *Intermedia 11*(4-5), pp. 18-21. © International Institute of Communications.

One notable trend is the different growth patterns of the media, patterns of growth that increase the imbalances between nations. Media experiencing slow growth were less evenly distributed among the nations to begin with. For example, most of the growth in the diffusion of computers occurred in the high-income nations. In 1987 the average penetration rate of personal computers in high-income nations was close to 200 times greater than in China and India. Newspaper circulation has also suffered a persistent decline, to a great extent because of the growth of television. This is a pattern found in all country categories. While the decline of newspaper circulation was worldwide, the decline was more precipitous in the low-income nations where newspaper circulation was already low.

The electronic media, on the other hand, are doing well. While radio has saturated the market in high-income nations, it has also reached a majority of the populations in even the poorest nations. Television is following a similar pattern and is emerging as the world's most popular communications medium. New media, including videocassette recorders, broadcast satellite, and cable television, have added to the increasingly rich world of video entertainment. In particular, videocassette recorders are thriving everywhere, defying hostile government regulations, religious practices, and poverty. On several Pacific Islands peasants often sell their land to buy the magic box.

These trends seem to point to an ever-widening gap between low-income nations (and to some extent, middle-income nations) and high-income nations in those information media that are seen as most important for informatization that leads to economic growth. This is not to say that the video media do not contribute to economic growth; certainly their information and advertising roles can have important political and cultural consequences. Perhaps the video media can stimulate development attitudes, but they can also create cultural divisions that hinder political and economic planning for growth.

Notes

1. The World Bank makes a distinction between lower-middle- and upper-middle-income countries. Because of data limitations, our comparisons must be broad rather than rigorous. We have, therefore, reduced this arrangement to three groupings—low-, middle-, and high-income nations—and will use the World Bank distinctions only when it is necessary to clarify a significant difference.

2. Joint ventures between Bell Atlantic and the city of St. Petersburg in Russia and between Bell Atlantic and Czechoslovakia for constructing local wired and cellular telephone systems are examples of steps taken to increase the diffusion of modern telecommunications in Eastern Europe.

3. Wilbur Schramm noted that in 1964, two-thirds of the world's population had one-third of the world's newspapers, one-quarter of the world's radio transmitters, and 12% of the world's television transmitters. See Schramm (1964).

4. The source of this data is the UNESCO *Statistical Yearbooks* of various years, used in the analysis that follows.

5. What little data Africa reports indicate very low rates of newspaper penetration. Rwanda, for example, at 0.1/1,000 in 1988. Interestingly, the former USSR has among the highest, if not the highest, newspaper penetrations of all nations, about 477/1,000.

6

How Does the Information Work Force
Contribute to Economic Growth?

Beginning in 1970, throughout the 1980s, and into the early 1990s we saw significant increases in the information work forces in almost all nations. We also encountered difficulties in defining just what information work and information workers are. Further, we found that too little attention has been given to the value of this work and the quality of the information work force; it has been tacitly assumed that information work is, by definition, high-value work and that information workers are, by definition, high-quality workers. In this chapter we examine these assumptions and also inquire into the relationship among information work, information workers, and economic growth. Just how does the information work force contribute to economic growth?

Economic Infrastructure

In our discussion of informatization (see Chapter 4) we defined three measures of economic parameters. These are (a) percentage of information workers in the nation's work force, (b) contribution of the information sector to the nation's GDP, and (c) contribution of the information sector to the productivity of the nation's industrial sector. We consider these measures in this chapter.

To date there have been few if any global analyses of these measures. Data for the developing nations are seldom available. Consequently, we examine a few selected nations—including developed and developing—and use this to provide an indication, but only an indication of global trends.

The Information Sector

In most of the high-income nations agriculture employment has long ceased to expand, and manufacturing employment has been declining, while the information sectors and service sectors (as they have been defined by various writers and discussed in Chapter 1) have been growing steadily. Appendix B, Table 7, shows the information sectors for eight highly industrialized, high-income nations from 1970 through 1989. By 1980 the sectors had all exceeded 40% of the work forces and increased rather steadily throughout the decade of the '80s and now stand at more than 45%, with three exceeding 50%. During the decade of the 1980s information work forces in these high-income nations increased by about 6%.

Most of the middle-income nations embarked on their paths toward the information economy somewhat later. Consequently, the size of their information work forces is smaller, ranging from slightly 35% of the total work force in Venezuela, Taiwan, and Republic of Korea in 1989, to 18% in Thailand for the same year (Appendix B, Table 7).

There are some very wide differences in the sizes of the information sector among the low-income nations; indeed, the information work forces in Egypt and the Philippines compare very favorably with those of the middle-income countries. Referring to Appendix B, Table 2, we see that the Per Capita Gross Domestic Product of these nations is considerably lower than that of Costa Rica, the ROK, or Brazil.

The relationship between the size of the information sector and economic growth is a key factor to understanding the importance of this sector to economic growth, and how informatization affects a nation's Gross Domestic Product. Oniki and Kuriyama provide some insight of the impact of information technology and the information industries on economic growth in Japan (Oniki & Kuriyama, 1989). By segmenting the value of produced goods and the capital stock into two components, one attributable to information technology and the other not attributable to information technology, they estimated the contribution of information technology to Japanese economic growth. The information technology component included the income gained from the value-added generated by the information industries and to the benefits of information products and services. These benefits, they suggest, led to a reduction in the cost of communications and coordination, hence, in management of the firms and to an increase in process and product quality. Oniki and Kuriyama estimated that the contribution of information technology to the Japanese economy from 1974 to 1985 could be in the range of 6.9% to 31.7% of the aggregate growth rate. Stated in another way, 0.64% of the Japan's 3.9% average annual growth rate is due to information technology. If there had not been investment in information technology, the level of Japan's GNP in 1985 would have been approximately 12% lower.

Jussawalla (1986) estimated the contribution of the information sector to other economic sectors in nine Pacific nations, using input-output analysis. Infrastructure construction and advertising in Fiji and Papua New Guinea generated demand in the business services and banking sectors. Similarly, the printing and paper industries in Australia created significant demand in those same sectors. It is interesting to note that even with a relatively small information work force, significant increases in economic growth during the late 1970s and early 1980s were found (Jussawalla, Lamberton, & Karunaratne, 1988). Jussawalla concluded that investments in selected primary information sector industries will stimulate growth in both the volume of industrial output and employment.

Similar to the findings in the nine Pacific nations, our study of information work forces in selected nations showed that, despite their relatively small information sectors, developing nations such as Thailand and Indonesia achieved a very respectable growth rate of more than 8% per year during the decade of the 1970s. On the other hand, despite its relatively large information sector, comparable to several middle-income countries, Egypt has not achieved similar rates of economic growth. Katz suggests that information workers in Egypt are likely to be employed in government providing health and welfare services, or are employed by government for political reasons, and those activities do not produce exports or goods that lead to economic growth (Katz, 1988). Government is often the employer of last resort.

Contribution of Information Sector
to Nation's GDP/Capita

A growing information sector does not necessarily lead to economic growth. Two additional measures have been devised to provide some insight into the degree to which the information sector does contribute to economic growth. Table 8 in Appendix B shows that for the high-income countries, there was a considerable increase in the degree to which the information sector appears to contribute to the GDP/capita of nations, from an average of 43% contribution in 1980 to 65% in 1988. This represents an increase of 51%. The nations perceived as being farthest along toward informatization—Japan, the United States, West Germany, and Canada—record significantly higher contributions of the information sector to the GDP/capita than did nations considered to be somewhat behind in the race toward informatization.

Among middle-income nations in Appendix B, Table 8, the increase in the contribution of the information sector to the nation's GDP/capita was less impressive, as compared to that in high-income nations, yet it too was significant. In Korea, for example, the contribution of the information sector to GDP was 14.6% in 1980. In 1988 the percentage doubled to 29.4%. The only exception in the upper-middle economies was Venezuela, where the contribution of its information sector to GDP/capita fell from 37.2% in 1980 to 27.3% in 1988. For most of the low-income economies in our sample there was no increase (indeed, a slight decrease) in the contribution of the information sector to the GDP/capita of these nations.

There are several reasons for these developments. Information infrastructures, mass media, telecommunications, and information technology must be available. They must be available to those sectors of the economy that contribute to GDP, such as manufacturing and the provision of exportable services and products. Finally, they must be effectively utilized. Therefore, when we consider the contribution of the information sector to the productivity of the manufacturing sector, we must take into account the nature of the work force in the information sector, the rate of literacy, and the number of school age population attending tertiary schools, which we discuss subsequently.

It is not only the size of the information sector that is important for effective informatization, but also the productivity of this sector. Jonschur (1983) tracked the productivity of information workers and attempted, by means of an econometric model, to predict future patterns of the size of the information sector. Jonschur argued that economic activity can be characterized as a production task and an information-handling task. Historically, the productivity of white-collar workers (information workers, for example), had been growing at a much slower pace than that of manufacturing or blue-collar workers. But as manufacturing adopts information technology, (computer-programmable processes, including robots and inventory control) higher speed and complexity will generate a need for more skilled manpower in handling the tasks of coordination and control, the information work. With the further introduction of information technology and skills training, this work force will, in time, stabilize or even decline as manufacturing productivity increases. The econometric model foresaw a "wall" beyond which the information sector would not grow, and that this "wall" in the United States was an information sector comprising 50% of the nation's work force.

Voge (1983) arrived at the same conclusion, but by other means. According to him the primary function of the information sector is the "organization and regulation of the socioeconomic system." Productivity is measured by the difference between the cost of production and that of organization. Voge found that since 1900 each time labor productivity grew by 10%, the information or organization costs per worker increased by 20%. When organization costs approach 50% of the GNP, productivity hits the "wall." Indeed, Voge found that the contribution of the information sector to the productivity of the economy begins to fall when the information sector passes 40% of the nation's work force. The reason for this is that productivity gains from modernization of facilities (informatization) are insufficient to offset the accompanying increase in training, research, and administrative costs. The United States reached this point in the mid-1960s, Europe in the 1970s.

Jonschur and Voge derived their forecasts by means of mathematical models stemming from historical data. Some confirmation of Voge's findings was found in a study of productivity in the finance and banking sector in New Zealand (Dordick, 1987, pp. 101-103). With its information sector at 35% of the of the nation's work force in 1980 and 40% in 1984, during this same period the dollar output per employee in the banking and finance sector experienced a dramatic decline, despite heavy investments in information technology during the previous decade.

Similar findings have been observed in the service industries in the United States as well. Beginning in the early 1970s this sector has reportedly invested between $600 and $800 billion on computerized equipment, including modern telecommunications. However, sector productivity fell from an average of 2.4% between 1947 and 1973 to 0.5% between 1973 and 1981. Beginning in 1982 and through 1985 productivity did increase to about 0.7% annually, as compared to the 4% annual growth rate for the manufacturing sector (*The New York Times,* 1987).

In the United States, the manufacturing sector has not fared much better, despite increases in automation. In 1987 alone, for example, an estimated $17 billion was spent on computers and new process-control equipment. As a result of this investment, productivity in the goods-producing industries grew at a rate of 3.5% for the decade of the 1980s, up from 1.4% during the period from 1973 to 1979. Examining productivity on a year-by-year basis shows that the growth began to slow, from a peak of 5% percent in 1983 to 3% in 1988 (Pennar, 1988).

Contribution of Information Sector
to Manufacturing Sector Productivity

Clearly, the contribution of the information sector to the manufacturing sector deserves to be examined in some detail. We have defined an indicator of this contribution in a highly aggregated manner, using data from readily available sources.

In most developed nations and in many developing nations, the labor force in the information sector has been growing and has exceeded that of the manufacturing and service sectors. There are problems in measuring the information and service sectors, and nations often have different definitions of which workers fit into which sectors. For this reason we do not claim that our analysis can be used to compare nations, but rather that it can be used to track progress toward informatization within a country. By some measures the United States has exceeded 50%, while Japan is approaching this figure. In contrast, other Asian countries have a relatively small portion of their labor in the information sector. There are significant exceptions: Singapore has a high percentage of workers in its information sector, perhaps as high as 46%, which is largely due to its heavy entrepot service sector and the fact that it is a compact city-state with no agricultural sector and a relatively small manufacturing sector.

We have chosen to simplify the enumeration of a nation's information sector; information labor force was calculated from the first four labor categories as defined in the in the *Yearbook of Labour Statistics*.[1]

Category 1: Professional, technical, and related occupations
Category 2: Administrative, technical, and related workers
Category 3: Clerical and related workers
Category 4: Sales workers

When compared to the disaggregate method of identifying information workers, as used by Porat and others, this aggregated approach results in an error of no more than ±4%. Similar results were obtained by Katz, who used the first three categories, which resulted in an error of between −3.5% for Germany in 1978 and 6.5% for Canada in 1951 (Katz, 1988, pp. 141-147).

With the manufacturing sector accounting for the majority of a nation's GNP (except in unusual economies such as Singapore) and more than 60% in 1988 in the United States, we have elected to determine the contribution of the information sector to the productivity of the manufacturing sector (U.S. Dept. of Commerce, 1991).

The contribution of the information sector to manufacturing sector productivity is determined by the ratio of the output of the manufacturing work force to the manufacturing labor force (actually, the logarithm of ratio).[2] The information sector contributes to the productivity of the manufacturing labor force by its more efficient coordination and control capabilities, at least in part by means of the information infrastructure.

Figure 6.1a shows the relationship between the contribution of the information sector to manufacturing sector productivity and the information sector for four ASEAN nations, Japan, Korea, and the United States for 1980, and Figure 6.1b for 1985. As one would expect, high productivity in the manufacturing sector is accompanied by a large information sector, indicating that the information labor force contributes significantly to manufacturing. Further, we note that the information sector grows twice as fast as manufacturing sector productivity, which suggests that Parkinson's (1980) findings are also true for the relationship between the growth of a nations's information sector and the growth of its GNP. As we noted previously he argues that this would lead to a leveling off of productivity gains with increases in the information labor force.[3]

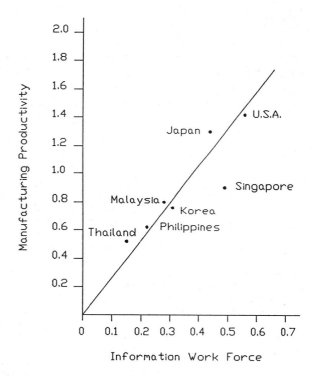

Figure 6.1a. Manufacturing Productivity vs. Information Work Forces (1980)

Evidence of this leveling off may be obtained from Table 9, Appendix B, for the United States during the period 1980 through 1989. Since 1980 the information labor force has made up more than 50% of the total work force. Despite this growth in the information sector, contribution to productivity in manufacturing had essentially leveled off, as is indicated in Figure 6.2.

Figure 6.3 provides the same information for Japan with dramatically different results. From 1982 onward, the information sector increased only marginally, yet there has been a dramatic increase in manufacturing productivity, especially in the years 1985 through 1988. (Further evidence for the period 1980 through 1988 can be seen in Table 9a, Appendix B.)

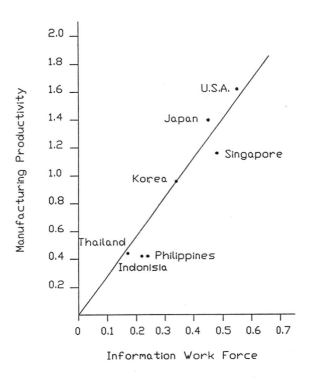

Figure 6.1b. Manufacturing Productivity vs. Information Work Forces (1985)

Figure 6.4 provides the same information for Korea, with results that are somewhat similar to that for Japan: modest growth in the information sector between 1985 and 1988 but a significant increase in manufacturing productivity, especially during the years 1987 and 1988 (refer also to Table 9, Appendix B).

We have examined the relationship between manufacturing productivity and information labor force for five of the six ASEAN nations. Singapore (Figure 6.5) exhibits a pattern that mildly parallels the Japanese experience: modest growth in the information sector and rather large growth in the productivity of the manufacturing sector (refer also to Table 9, Appendix B).

After an early drop in manufacturing productivity while the information sector was growing between 1980 and 1982, Thailand has shown

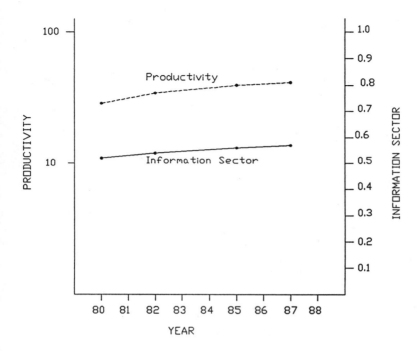

Figure 6.2. Manufacturing Productivity vs. Information Work Force—U.S.

a modest rise in this productivity, despite almost no growth in the information sector (refer to Table 9, Appendix B). This could be explained by an early investment in information workers for government and social service activities from the years 1980 through 1982; as social conditions improved between 1982 and 1988, these workers were then released to industry.

Malaysia (Table 9, Appendix B) exhibits stagnant growth in the information sector as well as in the productivity of the manufacturing sector. Why this is so is not clear, although Malaysia is developing an automobile industry using imported Japanese engines and other parts, presumably assembling the vehicles in Malaysia. Analysis of specific industries and specific firms is necessary to understand the Malaysian situation.

Finally, Indonesia and the Philippines (Table 9, Appendix B) show dramatic declines in manufacturing productivity while the information

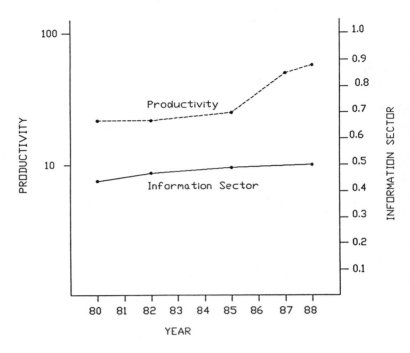

Figure 6.3. Manufacturing Productivity vs. Information Work Force—Japan

sectors have been modestly increasing. This may very well be another case in which the information sector is primarily engaged in government and social service activities, which may very well have been exacerbated during the years between 1982 through 1985. In the Philippines the period between 1982 and 1985 shows a very rapid decline in manufacturing productivity, which may very well be the consequence of political and economic turmoil during the excesses of the Marcos regime.

There is a strong relationship between the contribution of the information sector to the manufacturing sector and information sector growth and between both and the GDP/capita among the Group I high-income nations. The strength of these relationships tends to decrease for the middle-income nations and is considerably weaker for the lower-middle-

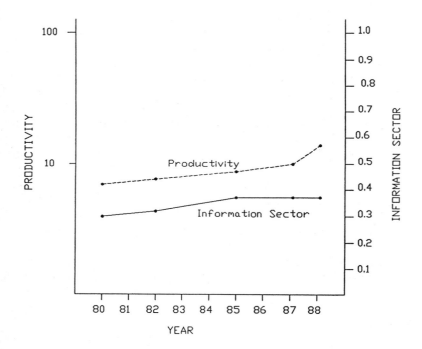

Figure 6.4. Manufacturing Productivity vs. Information Work Force—Korea

income and low-income nations. The reasons for these distinctions are both historical and structural.

It can be argued that the high-income nations emerged into the information society with a high level of manufacturing productivity even before the widespread adoption of information technology. Singapore is a special case of a nation that chose the informatization route in order to capitalize on its geographical location to become a center, indeed, an important node in the international trade and telecommunication routes for the West.

Among the middle-income nations, the Republic of Korea and Taiwan, the little tigers of Asia, are not entirely representative of this nation group, having elected to informatize as they rebuilt their industrial capacity in the 1970s and 1980s. However, they have in common

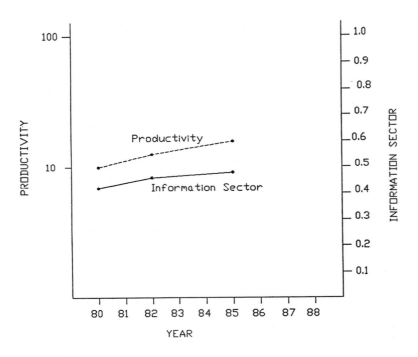

Figure 6.5. Manufacturing Productivity vs. Information Work Force—Singapore

with the other middle-income nations their relatively late arrival at the gates of the information era, but with the ability to take advantage of new information technology and modern telecommunications. During the early years of the 1970s, before their industrial capacity was sufficient to provide high levels of employment in manufacturing, employment in government jobs was required to maintain political peace and an economic safety net. This delayed the deployment of the information work force in industry and slowed productivity growth of that work force. Such was the case among many nations in the middle-income group.

Among the low-income countries, one finds a considerable portion of their information work forces engaged in government service tasks, thereby resolving potentially difficult political problems by providing this employment for serving the health and welfare needs of the poor and, to some extent, developing national infrastructures. Note that the information sectors in all of the selected nations in lower-middle-income and low-income nations exceed 20%; indeed, Egypt in 1988 reports that 33% of the nation's work force can be classified as information workers. And as expected, the contribution of this work force to manufacturing productivity and to the GDP/capita remains low. Only Thailand shows a trend toward higher productivity, greater GDP/capita, and a large contribution of its information work force to the GDP/capita.

The Service Sector

Many economists and other observers have noted that the service sector lags behind the manufacturing sector in productivity gains as a result of investments in information technology. Service sector productivity is difficult to measure. In banks, for example, there is the confusion between transaction productivity and information productivity. Bank officials are proud to announce that tellers can complete as many transactions in a 5-hour day as they formerly did in an 8-hour day, but also report that sales per employee have not significantly increased. Department store executives often state that while significant efficiencies have been made in inventory control and management, achieved by networking cash registers to inventory computers, "my sales people have forgotten how to sell" (see, e.g., Dordick, 1987; Dordick & Dordick, 1989).

A 1988 National Academy of Sciences study reported that while the goods-producing sector of the U.S. economy increased its productivity by 2.5 times the information technology investment, the service sector actually showed a reduction in productivity by about 0.3% from the period of 1973 to 1979 to the period of 1979 to 1985. The communications industry, with perhaps the largest investment in information technology, nevertheless exhibited sluggish productivity performance growth, 0.4% during these same periods (Roach, 1988).

Supporting the analysis above is yet another study of productivity growth versus investment in information technology in the United States, which found that productivity growth in business service, finance, insurance, and merchandising industries, as well as the manufacturing sector, has essentially stagnated, despite rapid adoption of information technology including modern telecommunications.[4]

There are also structural reasons for the lagging contributions of the information labor force to the GDP/capita and to productivity in the manufacturing sector: literacy and the level of tertiary education. We discuss these factors in the next chapter.

The Productivity Paradox

It appears that informatization can lead to economic development. But informatization is not the sole determinant of economic growth. This is evident from the differences in the consequences of informatization among the nation groups. Among the high-income nations, the parameters that determine the degree of informatization in a country do appear to lead to economic growth. Among the low-income nations, however, the impact of informatization is less dramatic and has not led to rapid economic growth. Indeed, it has often led to increased debt as they purchase information technologies and telecommunications equipment and systems.

Observers of contemporary economic trends are perplexed by the rapidity in the adoption of information technology and the relatively slow gains in productivity. In particular, this has been evident in the dramatic developments in information technology that have not appeared in the economic statistics of productivity. Paul David points out that this is not a new phenomenon, and that in 1900 observers may very well have said that electric dynamos were to be seen "everywhere but in the economic statistics," adapting Robert Solow's statement that "We see the computers everywhere but in the economic statistics" (David, 1989; see also Bailey & Gordon, 1980; Roach, 1983).

An OECD study notes that while the industrialized countries have built up a previously unequaled scientific and technological capacity, and technological change seems pervasive in everyday life, these countries appear to be finding it increasingly hard to translate this capacity into measurable productivity increases.[5]

We tend to overlook the fact that it takes time for new technology to be adopted by a firm. Training is required before use of these technologies is effective and, finally, the effective use of the new technology often requires structural changes in the firm.

David points out that it took almost a half-century for the productivity gains made possible by the dynamo to reach full fruition. Institutional change, continuing improvements of the dynamo that required changes in practices, also required almost continuous training and retraining. For the dynamo to achieve its full impact in society required wider adoption and this did not occur uniformly, even within a given plant. And we cannot overlook the general state of the economy.

To some extent we might apply similar reasoning to information technology, but we must be cautious because there are significant differences between the dynamo and the computer. Information has economic value when it is owned by a single person or firm. To avoid "information overload," which is derived from the improper use of information, often requires screening of information and intelligent decision about the information, and this costs money and requires skills that also cost money. Further, the complexity of the information technologies and the lack of standardization among their peripherals require time to debug and the skills to do so. Perhaps we are expecting too much too soon.

The Measurement Problem

Measuring productivity is fraught with danger. In this chapter we have used highly aggregated measures of productivity, recognizing the many inherent difficulties that have been encountered. More accurate and meaningful productivity measures must be highly focused on an individual firm or on a homogeneous industry, a group such as finance and banking. However, in these and other service industries, it is difficult to measure output. Sales cannot be used as output because products are not sold for money or for their full value. Consider, for example, government and nonprofit institutions, which together account for as much as 15% of the GDP, whose services are provided free or at a heavily subsidized price. In other cases, for example, finance, insurance, and real estate, there is no natural unit of output. In an effort to solve the problem in measuring productivity, the federal government equated the value of output to the cost of producing it. Panko (1990) argued that when output is growing at the same rate as input, productivity growth would always be zero, regardless of what is really happening.

The Gap Between the Rich and Poor Nations

The industrial countries we studied fared rather well in the 1980s, scoring moderate to high growth. Output was relatively high, unemployment was down, inflation was under control, and trade was expanding, having leaped across the "informatization barrier" in the early

1970s by rapid advances in the development of their information technology (and telecommunications), infrastructure growth in their information sectors, and enrollments in tertiary education, all of which led to productivity growth and resulting economic growth. In the early 1990s, growth slowed in the United States and other industrialized nations (except in Japan), and unemployment increased. It is likely to be more difficult for these nations to recapture the growth rates of the 1980s in the late 1990s and into the next century, but they will continue to dominate the global economy for some time to come.

Historic changes in the political systems in the Eastern European nations bode well for their economic growth, once political stability has been established and economic institutions rebuilt, along what is likely to be the social democratic lines found in Germany and other member nations of the Common Market. In their favor is an educational system that produces highly skilled professionals and workers. Among the middle-income nations in our sample, growth was rapid and sustained; the little tigers of Asia—the Republic of Korea, Taiwan, and Malaysia—led the group and have emerged as significant competitors of the high-income nations. Venezuela, Costa Rica, and Brazil are following in their footsteps. With the rising standard of living, jobs for information workers have shifted to manufacturing, thereby adding to economic growth.

During the 1980s there was some significant economic growth among the middle-income nations, with Malaysia and Indonesia benefiting from hosting U.S., Japanese, and European multinational firms. Indeed, the 1980s were a good decade even for sub-Saharan Africa, one of the world's poorest regions; growth in 1989 was strongest in the decade, at 3.5%. But with rapid population growth among these low-income countries, there was little change in per capita income. Indeed, per capita growth, even in the more prosperous, experienced a declining rate of growth.

During the 1980s the developing world in general did make significant progress in economic development and in the quality of life, as reflected in the growth of the information work force, the rate of literacy, and the percentage of the student population enrolled in tertiary education. Information infrastructures have also shown growth. However, the economic indicators of informatization have moved very slowly or not at all in many of the low-income nations. In part, lack of political stability is reflected in the lack of progress in manufacturing productivity and in the contribution of the information sector to the GNP/capita. This was very evident in the Philippines.

There are one billion people living on yearly incomes of less than $370, the poverty level as defined by the World Bank (World Bank, 1990). And despite efforts by the United Nations Industrial Development Organization to increase the share of manufacturing by the developing nations (a goal of a 25% share was set for the year 2000), and an average of more than $20 billion per year in grants, by 1988 the Third World nations' share in industrial output was only 13.8% (excluding China), 3.8% greater than it was in 1970. And despite efforts to adopt policies of informatization and expensive investments in information technology and modern telecommunications, while export trade in the industrialized nations continued to grow, that of the developing nations continued to decrease, signifying a shrinking share in international trade.

It is evident that the process of informatization demands a long-term commitment in capital, both equipment and human. Having made this investment, nations achieved significant rates of economic growth. This is evident among the high- and middle-income countries. The low-income nations do not have the capital resources to make the long-term investments required to accelerate their growth and, consequently, cannot develop the professional and skilled talents required for informatization for economic growth. Indeed, many of the poorer nations cannot even embark on the road to informatization; they lack the basic infrastructures on which to base economic growth and the possibility of improved standard of living, including power, water, and transportation.

In this chapter we examined the size of the information work force, the contribution of the information sector to economic growth, and manufacturing productivity in a number of selected nations. What we have discovered confirms, in part, the contribution of the information sector in economic growth, but at the same time calls for a review of theoretical statements and policy decisions that make blanket assumptions regarding such contribution, a point which we will elaborate in Chapter 8.

Notes

1. Data from the *Yearbook of Labour Statistics* of various years, published by International Labour Office (ILO), Geneva.

2. Sources are *Yearbook of Labour Statistics ILO*, various years, and *The World Development Report*, World Bank, various years.

3. Voge reminds us of Parkinson's "square law" phenomenon for large organizations, in which organizations grow faster than the productive output of these organizations.

4. Dordick and Dordick (1989) add to this rather bleak picture that despite the world's second-largest proportion of scientists and engineers (the former Soviet Union was the first), the number of patents granted to U.S. investors steeply declined from 1972 to 1979, rose slightly in 1981, and entered into another decline in 1982, from which it is now slowly recovering. At the same time, the number of patents granted for foreigners, Japan and West Germany, has been steadily increasing since 1968.

5. OECD: CSTP Programme, 1989, p. 1.

7

Information Technology
and Social Change:
Beyond Infrastructure
and Economic Growth

Informatization concerns social development for which infrastructure is indispensable. In this chapter the social parameters discussed in Chapter 4 are discussed. In this chapter we are primarily concerned with the individual in the information society. We seek to find out whether the important societal changes, primarily in the way we conduct our daily lives, that were forecast decades ago have taken place.

Some of these purported changes, for example, high levels of production and consumption of information, were central to the theory of information society we discussed in Chapter 2. Others, including the way we teach and learn, and that elusive relationship between travel and communications embodied in the concept of "telecommuting," or bringing the work to the worker rather than the worker to the work, were to be the rewards of informatization. Additionally, shorter working hours allowing more time for the spiritual were seen as an ideal consequence of informatization. According to the utopians, it is because of changes such as these that we forecast not merely an information industry or information sector, but a societal future distinctly different from the past. Social transformations do not occur in a few decades, and it may be too early to draw conclusions concerning a future society. Indeed, in this age of rapid change, any forecasting is risky. However, certain trends are observable, trends that might very well indicate radical changes in society that are difficult to ignore. We shall not draw conclusions, but rather make sense of the observed trends.

Information Production and Consumption

Masuda suggested that the driving force of an information society is the production and consumption of information. Certainly, in order to produce and consume, information tools and transport mechanisms are necessary: information technology and telecommunications.

Just how much information is available to the citizens of a nation and how much is actually consumed? While one may have serious reservations with the measures used in the only two research projects undertaken to consider this question, it is useful to inquire into this ratio in the two countries that are the prime members of the information society club, Japan and the United States.

Japanese researchers concluded that between 1975 and 1984 the quantity of information produced, telecommunications, mass media, postal service, and face-to-face communication (as classroom lectures and conferences) more than doubled (*Telecommunications White Paper*, 1990). Figure 7.1 shows that information produced by telecommunication and electronic media are leading all sources of information and, in 1988, reached 98.9% of the total growth.

The quantity of information consumed during the same period of rapid information production grew much slower. However, the consumption of telecommunications and electronic information experienced sluggish growth in the mid-1980s and in 1982 actually began to fall behind print and the post, which scored a steady increase during these years. In 1988 consumption of information transmitted over telecommunications and electronic media accounted for 62.2% of the total amount, followed by face-to-face communication, which accounted

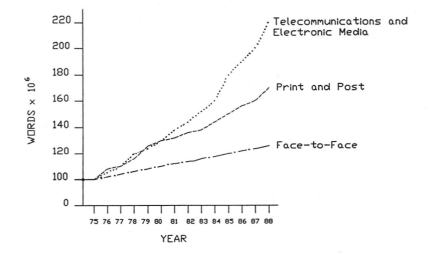

Figure 7.1. Information Production in Japan
SOURCE: *Telecommunications White Paper*, Tokyo: Ministry of Post and Telecommunications, 1990.

for 34.1%, and postal services, which accounted for 3.7% (Figure 7.2). Face-to-face communication accounted for no more than .06% of the total information supply, but accounted for 34.1% of total information consumption. With the advent of cable television, which can supply hundreds of channels, this supply and consumption gap is expected to widen.

Even with these findings, RITE found very little change in household information expenditure and information utilization in Japanese households, although the cost of information has steadily decreased. As a result of the rapidly falling cost of semiconductor technology, there was a significant increase in household information equipment. Ithiel Pool and his associates (Pool et al., 1984) essentially repeated this research in the United States in order to compare it with the Japanese results. Figure 7.3 compares the annual growth rate per capita of the supply and consumption of information in the United States and Japan.

The volume of words produced in Japan and the USA has been growing about 2.5 times as fast as the volume consumed. From 1960 to 1980 the words made available to Americans through the various media grew at a rate of 8.8% per year, or more than double the 3.7% per year growth rate for the nation's GNP. The supply of words in the United

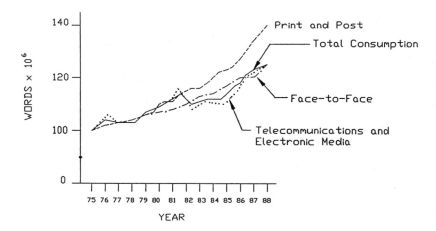

Figure 7.2. Information Consumption in Japan

SOURCE: *Telecommunications White Paper*, Tokyo: Ministry of Post and Telecommunications, 1990.

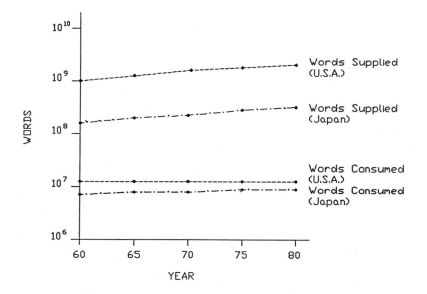

Figure 7.3. Supply and Consumption per Capita

SOURCE: *Communication Flows: A census in the United States and Japan* (p. 19) by I. de S. Pool et al., Tokyo: University of Tokyo Press, 1984.

States is significantly greater than that for Japan, a reflection of the extent of radio and television viewing in the United States. Interestingly, while television viewing reduced radio listening in the United States, the introduction of television had a much more dramatic effect in Japan, significantly reducing total words supplied. Pool remarks that the lower information consumption rate in the United States that occurred in the mid-seventies resulted from the tapering off of television viewing, which had not yet occurred in Japan but would probably take place in the last years of the 1970s (Pool et al., 1984).

Similar research has not been performed elsewhere. But Japan and the United States are considered forerunners in the race toward informatization, and it is useful to speculate on implications for other societies when they reach similar levels of development. Clearly, we can foresee an ever-widening gap between information production and information consumption. As a greater percentage of the work force becomes engaged in information work, and information technology continues to provide greater and greater capacity for processing, storing, and transmitting, information supply can be expected to grow. Is there a limit to this growth? Is the limit one of market demand? It was not very long ago when the Federal Communications Commission considered abandoning the licensing of additional communication satellites, arguing that there already was an excess of transponders or bandwidth available. In like manner, it was argued that the number of cable television channels might well not need to grow beyond 30 in the United States; viewers generally select from no more than 8 channels. Yet today, the number of satellite transponders increases and the number of cable channels offered increases. In the case of video, bandwidth offered is always filled. As the cost of information production and its distribution decreases, there seems to be no end in sight for continued increases in the production of information. And much the same is true in the print media.

Time, however, does limit the consumption of information for the individual. There are only so many hours in the day when the individual can read, view television, listen to music, talk to others, read postal or electronic mail, and so forth. Further, while information can be produced at a very rapid rate, it can be consumed at a relatively slow rate. We have not yet developed the means nor the capacity to efficiently select and organize information for our consumption. Consequently, we often hear about "information overload."

If there is to be a limit on the production of information, it will be driven by the market demand, which in turn will be determined by the ability of people to utilize this information effectively and enjoyably. This limit will, to a considerable degree, be determined by the rate of literacy and level of education in the society. This brings us to a discussion of the social parameters of our measure of informatization, and how and if informatization has reached the individual in school, in the workplace, and in the home.

Literacy

In our measures for informatization we have selected rate of literacy and percentage of tertiary school students in their respective age groups as social measures of informatization, for the reasons noted in Chapter 4. Clearly, the effective utilization of information requires a literate population. Furthermore, to maintain high standards of living requires the production of high-value services and products and high-wage workers. It is the quality as well as the quantity of jobs that makes for a growing economy. Quality work can only be performed by well-trained, literate, educated workers. That this is so, consider the literacy rate reported by the high-income nations, all of whom are often considered as highly informatized (See Appendix B, Table 10). The data is scattered across the years, but with the exception of Singapore, every nation reports almost 100% literacy.[1]

There is a wide range of variations among the developing nations; for example, the rate of literacy in Costa Rica is more than 93%, but only 44% in India. For the middle-income nations, the rate of literacy was estimated to be over 80% in 1985. Taiwan and the Republic of Korea, the little tigers of Asia, had the highest rates of literacy, at 95% and 92%, respectively. But for the lower-income nations, the rate of literacy of the population averaged about 30%, with some nations reaching a high of 45%. India and China alone account for 55.5% of the world's illiterate population (UNESCO, 1988, p. 17).

There is ample evidence that high levels of literacy are important national objectives. From 1970 to 1985, the worldwide average literacy rate rose from 65% to 73%, a significant improvement, considering a population growth of 30% during the same period. The most impressive improvement was in the high-income nations, where the rate of literacy rose, on the average, from 72% in 1970 to 87% in 1985. Literacy rates among the low-income nations also rose from an average of 30% in 1970 to 44% in 1985. Among middle-income nations, rates of literacy have also increased but at a slower rate than among the high-income nations, from an average of 71.5% in 1970 to an average of 73% in 1985. The Philippines have, traditionally, had a relatively high-quality educational system, modeled on that of the United States, and this is reflected in its rate of literacy, which is well above the average for the group.

Tertiary Education

Literacy has been used as an indicator for a basic level of education. But in an information age, literacy is not sufficient to ensure a high-quality work force; higher education is needed. A useful measure is the percentage of students attending tertiary school in their age groups (see Table 11, Appendix B). UNESCO data for 1987 reported that the percentage of college students has reached 30% of their age group among the high-income nations. For the middle-income nations, the average percentage of students in the school age group was 15%, and for low-income nations, 1.5%. It is interesting to note that the two nations that are often ranked as the most informatized have very different rates of tertiary school attendance: 28% in Japan and more than 60% for the United States in 1985, the year for which we have the best data.

On the other hand the percentage in a number of Asian nations was found to be at a level similar to that of high-income nations. Among middle-income nations, the Republic of Korea reports more than 36% of tertiary school attendance. Once again the Philippines stands out; the percentage was 38%, although its per capita income was considerably lower than that of Korea.

Informatization in Our Daily Lives

Education

In 1988 the working group of the International Federation for Information Processing (IFIP) enumerated five reasons why computers should be used in education (IFIP, 1988):

> To individualize instruction, in order to better deal with individual differences among students. With appropriate software a student can become a self-directed and self-initiating learner.
> To contribute to learning mastery. The appropriately programmed can be used to select alternative learning paths on the basis of the student's past records, and monitor the progress of each individual student.

> To make higher quality material available more widely. With the
> expansion of broad-band information networks, sharing of quality instruc-
> tional materials and software packages among educational institutions
> becomes easier and financially viable.
>   To emphasize analysis and logical thinking, a major weakness of many
> learners. The computer's requirement for precise and ordered logic pro-
> vides an ideal opportunity for training in logical thought.
>   To stimulate educational reform. The computer allows for the satisfac-
> tion of individual learning needs. Institutions can create a more flexible
> environment to supplement students' instructions at the home, in small
> groups or in learning centers.

There are, of course, many other roles for information technology in
education. The technology "so versatile, so rich in possibilities, that
virtually any view of what education is or ought to be can be imple-
mented" ("The use," 1984).

A major objective of informatization is the training of a work force
capable of effectively using information in the high-value jobs that will
be necessary to achieving higher standards of living in the information
era. Perhaps the term *computer literacy* best describes the knowledge
and skills required in order to work with computers and other information technologies. These skills involve more than the ability to program
or use computers; it is "the stage in which there would be fundamental
innovation in conceptualizing and processing information. This would
involve a shift in perception about information formats and uses as
fundamental as the shift from memory to written records was as the
basis for traditional literacy" (Compain, 1988). With this as a back-
ground, we examine where information stands today in the process of
reaching the social goal of a literate, and a computer literate, work force
for the next century.

Several governments have been the major promoters of computer
literacy programs. Servan-Schreiber (1979) encouraged the French
government to establish broad policies to lead the nation into the
computer age, the age of *informatique*. There has been federal and state
funding for more than 2 million personal computers for the nation's
classrooms in the United States, a nation that disavows social policy
(U.S. Dept. of Commerce, 1991). China allocated approximately 0.02%
of its annual budget for educational technology, a considerable investment for a low-income nation (UNESCO, 1987). Funds provided by
loans and gifts from the advanced nations enabled Jordan and India to

embark on computer literacy programs. Zimbabwe created a regional training center for African nations, including Ethiopia, Malawi, Mozambique, Zambia, and others (Hawkridge, Jawarski, & McMahon, 1990).

In 1985 some 7,000 educational packages were on the market, with 100 to 150 new ones added to the list every month. Many of these programs claim to be able to "teach" year-long courses in geometry and algebra with an effectiveness "approaching" that of a human tutor (Chaiklin & Mathews, 1988). However, questions remain about just how effective information technology is in the educational process.

Numerous studies have shown diverse results. For example, some teachers saw their role in computer-using classes as less teacher-centered, thereby allowing for individualized relationships. Classes seem to be more cooperative, with higher student interest. Students who had word-processing and/or programming skills reported better grades than those who lacked those skills (Smith & Zimmerman, 1988).

A number of other studies, revealed:

- Stronger short-term, rather than long-term effect of computer-based instructions.
- Computers cannot replace conventional teaching but rather support that teaching.
- Improved software is crucial and its introduction showed significant improvements in student performance.
- Students who have used computers report more positive attitudes toward school and their subjects. (Kulik, 1986)

It is not possible, however, to generalize these findings; indeed, Kulik concluded that the effect of computer-based teaching differs at different instruction levels. For example, computer-based mathematics teaching did raise examination scores, but did not do so at higher levels or in other subjects.

Just how informatization can assist in education is still unclear; but what is clear is that the availability of information resources and an information infrastructure for a more equitable distribution of these resources is a necessary prerequisite (Martinez & Mead, 1988).

Despite significant investments in the information technologies, while 96% of public schools in the United States had at least one computer, most had no more than 20 in their school for an entire student population that often numbered more than 2,500 students. This number has not significantly increased in the years since. In Japan, statistics told a similar story: 56.4% of the upper secondary schools had computers, but only 2% had more than 20 microcomputers, and most had fewer than 3. At the elementary school level, more than 80% of the students had no experience in using computers (Shiba, 1986).

As in so many other aspects of informatization, achieving the goals sought goes far beyond merely having the tools. Information technology merely provides an opportunity to achieve goals, permits goals to be reached. Indeed, we suggest that information technologies, including telecommunications, are permissive technologies. Perhaps the missing link is that we do not have any solid theories of learning that the technologies can build upon. Learning is a process that requires a change in behavior, and to date we know no better way to achieve the desired behavioral changes than by face-to-face interaction between teacher and student. Effective and wise use of technology can assist the teacher in shaping his or her day in a way that allows more time for attention to individual students. Information technology, then, might well be seen as playing a greater logistics role, rather than a teaching role.

In Daily Life

How has the emerging informatization of society affected our daily lives, the way we work and perform necessary chores? It is this question that has brought forth the most imaginative and futuristic writings about the information society. Information technology will facilitate education and work. Automation made possible by the use of intelligent computers and rapid and highly efficient communications will liberate us from routine tasks. Work hours will be shorter, and ultimately we will have more time for self-actualization and spiritual growth. An electronic marketplace will emerge that will bring work and daily tasks to us in our homes, thereby relieving cities of the burden of traffic and pollution.[2]

Since the early 1970s, more than 70 studies have been published on the topic of telecommuting, including several that surveyed corporations attempting to engage employees in teleworking. Just what is a "teleworker"? The United States Census defines a teleworker as one who worked at home on an income-producing job for at least 8 hours per week. By this definition, there were 23 million teleworkers in the United States in 1989 (Kraut, 1989).

If the term is limited to those who use their home as the primary workplace for their primary job, this number is drastically reduced to about one million (Kraut, 1989). It is assumed that this work is made possible by the availability of information technology and modern telecommunications, and to a considerable extent, this is the case. However, a survey of teleworkers found that more than 70% of the respondents relied on postal services, and up to 80% communicated by letters and other paper-based documents. Less than one-third used courier service to send tapes or diskettes, and three-quarters regularly attended face-to-face meetings away from their homes. Teleworking is defined more in terms of the location of work than the use of information networks. Indeed, many work at home one or more days per month in order to be free of the telephone and other information technologies (Di Martino & Wirth, 1990; Huws, Kort, & Robinson, 1990).

Few workers choose the work-at-home option unless compelled to by illness or family situations such as the need to care for young children. There are relatively few jobs, other than consulting, professional work, or telemarketing, that are suitable for home work. Despite the continuing enthusiasm futurists display concerning the substitution of communications for transportation, business centers continue to crowd with executives and workers who find it necessary and desirable to "press the flesh." And family health seems to require the separation of the work space from the home space.

Unexpected Consequences

The United States meets the criteria for being an information society. More than half of its work force is in the information sector; the rate of literacy is at about 100%; almost 60% of the school age population attends tertiary schools; and telephone and broadcast services are essentially universally available.[3] The contribution of its information sector to the nation's Gross Domestic Product ranks second only to Japan. And while productivity in the manufacturing sector has been stagnant for several years, it is still among the highest in the industrialized world.

Yet, people are working longer hours than ever before; unemployment among information workers is high and will probably remain so for some years to come; and the workplace has not been humanized (Schor, 1992).

Machines have replaced human labor, and it was anticipated that the work week would gradually decline. After World War II it was expected that the work week would be 35 hours. When computers and computer-related systems and products arrived on the scene, human labor was to become less routine and tedious. What to do with leisure time would become an issue, and universities would have to provide departments of leisure studies. Automation and computerization on the factory floor were supposed to release workers from the tyranny of machines and from Taylorism. Around 1970 the normal American work week, after gradually declining to about 39 hours, began increasing. In the 20 years since, the years during which an information economy fully blossomed in the United States, working time has steadily increased to the point where the average worker now puts in an estimated 168 extra hours of paid labor a year, the equivalent of an additional month of work each year. There has been a 40% decline in a person's free time since 1973. Almost 40% of households in the United States have dual wage earners, usually an employed mother who works an average of 65 hours per week, including housework, child care, and employment. More than 30% of fathers with children under 14 work 50 or more hours per week. Computers seem to control workers in a subtle way, monitoring workers quietly and persistently.

Hard economic times no longer affect only the blue-collar worker, the unskilled worker, and the semiskilled worker, but appear to have hit middle management hardest, not only on the United States but throughout the industrialized countries as well. Consider, what do middle managers do? A middle manager communicates and coordinates. Networked computers can do the same. Hence, the information era has brought corporate downsizing to a new level of sophistication; middle managers in the thousands have been laid off, made redundant. Following the AT&T divestiture, the first major layoffs were 15,000 middle level managers.

The global market was made possible by modern telecommunications and information technology. Corporate downsizing has become the means for improving profits and remaining competitive, and labor has become just another commodity to be downsized. The alternative, increasing the productivity of the workers and making certain that technology is used effectively to achieve increased productivity, costs money—and downsizing does not. And workers do the work of two over longer hours.

The labor movement in the United States was a major force for shorter work hours and improved work conditions. But computer-controlled manufacturing, office management, and coordination and communications require fewer people, and you do not unionize machines or computers. Worldwide data communication allows firms to export work to low-labor-cost countries and manage remotely. Labor knows no national boundaries, and neither does capital.

Living standards have stagnated, and families feel trapped by higher living costs and either shorter work hours or work at minimum-wage salaries. The two-worker-income household has become commonplace, and women and men find themselves under greater time pressure at home as well as in the workplace. Machines in the kitchen have meant more work for mother. And in about one-third of the households in the United States, a member works at least 8 hours per week for pay at home, perhaps at a second job.

For the past 40 or more years, the household communications environment has been controlled by outside forces: broadcast television, the insistent and disconcerting phone call at the wrong time, and the plague of wrong numbers or abusive callers. We have dinner after the evening news, go to sleep after the late evening news, or lose sleep to watch a late-night talk show. Families now want to control their household communications environment.

Information technologies abound in homes, especially among young families, with or without children. More than 95% of these families have a VCR; more than one-third have a personal computer and, of these, almost one-fifth communicate or access databases remotely; one-third have compact disc players; and there are answering machines in 50% of these young households. These families purchase a number of telephone devices that enhance their communications capability or control access to them, including the ability to conference, to forward calls to another number, and the like. New technologies, such as voice mail, the videophone, personal communications, database access, and caller identification, are likely to be favorably received (Dordick & LaRose, 1992).

This concentration of information services and devices seeks to recreate the separation of family life from civil life, and return control to the individual and the family. Further, these technologies offer the ability to manage information consumption and enhance information production. Information technologies are not restricted to the young, although they tend to be early adopters because they enjoy keeping up with their peers. Among families with seniors, between the ages of 65 and well beyond 70, there is extensive use of information technology and the likelihood that these seniors will purchase such new technologies, including the videophone, voice mail, and such safety features as fire alarm and burglar alarm services.

Even low-income households have a high interest in some of these services, contradicting the naysayers who would have us believe that new information technologies are irrelevant or even harmful to the public. And a surprising number of people of all ages and income levels are seriously interested in the technologies that enable them to talk on the telephone while simultaneously sending or receiving facsimile messages and data. With less free time, people appear to want to make the most of this time, not just for relaxation or self-improvement but also for unpaid activities that a viable society requires, from civic participation to voluntary caring for young and old.

Multinational firms headquartered in five industrialized nations dominate the information and telecommunications equipment and system markets. Research, development, and advanced computing applications and software are rarely, if ever, performed in the host countries. Anxious not to fall too far behind the developed nations, developing countries search for capital to invest in information technology. But the gap between the have and the have-not nations continues to grow, rapidly and constantly.

Cities are still searching for the magic trade-off between telecommunications and transportation, in the hope of stemming gridlock traffic in center cities and poisonous air pollution. But people like people and do not seem ready to work away from their co-workers, and they recognize that absence from the supervisor does not make his or her heart grow fonder. Information technology and modern telecommunications enable firms to locate wherever they wish, wherever they find skilled workers at the right price. It just happens that good labor is often found in major cities; there is a clear relationship between the cultural excitement and the educational opportunities in the city and the availability of good workers. Opera, baseball, football, theaters, and concerts via television only increase the number of people who wish to see and hear the real thing.

We continue to have faith in progress. It is embedded very deeply in our culture. We continue to believe that our lives are better than those that came before us, and that our children's lives will be better than ours. Today, this faith appears to be placed on information and the society we are producing to make the most of its promise for the good life.

Notes

1. This data should be considered with several caveats. Singapore is, essentially, a multilingual society: Malay, Chinese (both Mandarin and Cantonese), and English. A national movement is under way to designate Mandarin Chinese as the national language, with English a second language. Consequently, it is not clear if Singapore's data on literacy considers only Mandarin Chinese speakers.

2. The number of published works that have expounded these ideas is much too large to list. The earliest proponent, and probably the most imaginative and articulate, remains Yoneji Masuda, to whom we have frequently referred (Masuda, 1981). See also Dordick, Bradley, & Nanus (1981).

3. There is considerable dissatisfaction with this figure provided by the U.S. Census. Observers of the education and training scene in the United States argue that a more meaningful measure would be one of functional literacy, usually meaning the ability to read at a fifth-grade level. And this figure is 80%, they say.

8

Reading the Trends

In Retrospect

In our opening chapter we asked if we are, indeed, entering a new age, the information age. We asked if this is the cusp of a global information economy and information society to which all nations are striving, and if it is, how well are they doing? And just what does the information society mean to the citizens of these nations?

We embarked on a retrospective view to see where we have been and what have been the consequences of the promises made and the plans carried out. Has a global economy, caught in the web of modern telecommunications and information technology, emerged? And what has been the impact on both the industrializing and industrialized nations? In particular, what has been the impact of informatization on the individual, and have we learned from our experience in the Industrial Revolution over the past 200-plus years to utilize new technologies more efficiently, humanely, and ethically?

Answers are not simple; the informatization and economic processes are complex, and there is always insufficient data. Even for the information we do have, it was difficult to understand its meaning. Meaning requires understanding relationships, and with this understanding, one should be able to clarify some of the mysteries regarding the future. But when dealing with society, the signs are mixed at best. In this chapter we try to make some sense of what we found, and venture a revised picture of the future.

What the critical qualities of an information society are cannot be answered to everyone's satisfaction. Some would see such a society as one in which repetitive, routine, and dull work will be performed by computer systems or robots, a society in which one can attend to intellectual and scholarly wants rather than tasks to satisfy needs. Others might see such a society as one in which only high-value jobs are worth performing, thereby leaving time for leisure and learning, leading to a high standard of living. But is an information society one in which those not capable of performing high-value work are unemployable and are relegated to empty, meaningless, low-income tasks that even computers cannot perform?

Nor can what constitutes an information society be universally defined by a simple set of criteria. Japan's RITE made this attempt.[1] Lack of or sparse data from many countries exposes the shortcoming of this measure as well as many other measures that seek ease of definition. Working with available data only, we would have to say that only two nations, the United States and Canada, satisfy RITE's criteria for admittance to the information society club; Japan, with only 28% of its school age population attending tertiary schools, would not qualify!

When we look at other aspects of informatization in the United States and Canada, however, the picture becomes blurred. In the United States information consumption has scored only moderate growth, and its information sector has not yet accounted for a major share of the nation's GDP. In addition, despite wide application of information technologies, many of the social changes that were expected to follow failed to appear: Telecommuting remains the working style of a minority of workers; computers have not yet revolutionized education; and automation has not brought shorter work hours.

The World According to Informatization Indicators

To examine informatization we developed three sets of parameters for our study: infrastructure, economic, and social measures. We found in general that what was forecast decades ago was confirmed; there has been significant growth in all three dimensions in almost all nations for which data was available. The confirmation, however, is not without limitations. Some changes that were key to the information society concept did not appear, but others that were not forecast did. In the trend of development, at least three areas are worthy of attention: (a) the contribution of the information infrastructure, including literacy and tertiary education, to economic growth; (b) the contribution of the information work force to economic growth; and (c) disparities among nations.

Information Infrastructures and Economic Growth

We defined the information infrastructure as consisting of the mass media: television and newspapers, telephones, computers and other data terminals. While the causal link between economic growth indicators and communications eludes us, there is some evidence that a significant correlation exists between them. Because of sparse data we can only make this statement for specific years.

Taking all of our sample nations as a group, we found that Gross Domestic Product per capita appeared to correlate well with radio, television, and telephone penetration and newspaper circulation during the 1980s among all nations in our sample (see Table 8.1). Correlations among selected groups were more difficult because of the lack of sufficient data. However, we found that for the high-income nations, year-by-year correlation was much weaker, confirming our earlier analysis concerning the relationship between television and GDP/capita. We noted previously that the diffusion of radio and television leveled off, but GDP/capita continued to increase. Saturation of these media in the high-income nations appears to have occurred. We expect that television and GDP/capita would be strongly related in the middle- and low-income nations in which television penetration is low and is continuing to increase.

As the telephone penetration increased in the high-income nations, the strength of the correlation between telephone penetration and GDP/capita weakened, as it had for television growth. Among middle-income nations telephone penetration and GDP/capita correlated quite closely during the period of 1980 through 1989.

Newspaper penetration also appears to correlate quite strongly with GDP/capita when the countries are taken as a whole. Among the high-

Table 8.1 Correlation Between GDP/Capita and Media Penetration

Year	Television	Radio	Newspaper	Telephone	Tertiary Ed.
			Measure of Correlation (r)		
1970	.93**	.81**	.81**	.90**	.79**
1980	.73**	.58**	.91**	.72**	.51**
1981	.79**	.61**	—	.84**	.55**
1982	.77**	.60**	.84**	.76**	.56**
1983	.83**	.61**	—	.79**	.68**
1984	—	—	.83**	.80**	.63**
1985	.79**	.67**	—	.83**	.61**
1986	.81**	.71**	.85**	.89**	.65**
1987	.81**	—	—	.89**	.65**
1988	—	—	.91**	—	—
1989	.79**	.69**	.94**	—	—

** $p < .01$

income nations, the decline in newspapers per 1,000 population has had little bearing on GDP/capita. Among middle-income nations, there is evidence of a relationship between newspaper circulation and GDP/capita. The data for the low-income nations is much too sparse to draw any statistical conclusions, but newspaper circulation appears to have declined and GDP/capita to have grown very slowly.

Even the sparse data presented and analyzed here support the notion that per capita GDP and television, newspaper, and telephone penetration are positively related, thereby strengthening, once again, the dominant paradigm as restated in the 1980s and described in Chapter 2. That paradigm argued that the mass media, including telecommunications, may very well stimulate economic growth. Further, significant correlations between per capita income and the telephone in the middle-income nations support the importance of the telephone to economic growth.

The number of computers and data terminals on telephone and telex networks may represent the most visible aspect of informatization. Yet data is lacking and, where available, may present only part of the story. As noted in the previous chapter, nations are increasingly permitting private networks for firms with heavy data communication needs. These data terminals are not reflected in the data currently collected by international as well as national agencies.

Despite this handicap we find a strong relationship between the amount of data terminal equipment on the public telephone and telex networks and GNP/capita for the eight developed nations. There is insufficient data to determine any relationship for the developing nations. However, there is a strong relationship between the growth of data terminals and GDP/capita in Malaysia. One also finds a modest correlation between data communications and GDP/capita for Thailand and the Philippines.[2]

The mass media, telecommunications and computers, and other data terminals are important for economic growth. That this relationship is strongest among high-income nations is not surprising, given their capacity to purchase this equipment and the availability of skilled workers. It is not surprising to find the middle-income nations also exhibiting a relationship between the availability of information technology and economic growth, although somewhat weaker than that of the high-income nations, due to their later start and limited supply of trained workers in their information work force. Further, many of the information workers are engaged in work to meet the nation's social service needs in the face of lagging standards of living. Among the low-income nations there is a much weaker relationship between investments in information technology and economic growth, primarily because of their limited resources for purchasing these systems and equipment and their meager trained work force. While correlations between telephone, television, newspaper, and per capita GDP lend support to theories of development communications, the strength of these correlations in low-income nations suggests that technology is necessary but not sufficient for stimulating economic growth. Whether and how information technology contributes to economic growth is of critical interest to policymakers, and promoting informatization is an expensive endeavor, and for nations with limited resources, a risky decision. Purchasing technology requires hard dollars and provides a return only if there are educated and trained workers to use this technology. Planning for the effective utilization of information technology, including the mass media, is long-range.

Because educated and trained workers are so important to the efficient use of infrastructure, it makes good sense to examine here the contribution of literacy and tertiary education to economic growth. It is impossible to report a statistically meaningful relationship between literacy and economic growth; there are so many other human factors that affect the relationship between these factors. Certainly low rates of literacy may add to political instability, which, in turn, has a significant impact on economic growth.

However, the level of school age population attending tertiary schools may very well be a contributing determinant to slow rates of informatization, which leads to sluggish economic growth. There is a modest correlation between tertiary education and the productivity contributions of the information sector to manufacturing among high-income and middle-income nations, and a weaker correlation among lower-middle-income and low-income nations. Further, higher rates of literacy clearly can lead to higher rates of tertiary school attendance. However, the data obtained can only provide us trends or indicators, rather than directionality correlation between these variables. A higher standard of living will lead to increased literacy rates as well as greater levels of attendance in tertiary schools (Table 8.1).

The Contribution of the Information Work Force to Economic Growth

Machlup, Masuda, Porat, and Bell argued that information- and knowledge-based activities will become the driving forces in the future societies they called postindustrial or information societies. We found growing information work forces in every country we examined, from the high-income nations to the low-income nations. But we also found differences in how the information sector was defined, and in the nature of the work performed in these sectors. We resolved the former difficulty by using the first four categories in the International Labour Organization's classification of information workers in our measurement of the information sector in all of the countries we examined.

What is more important, however, is the nature of the work performed by this sector. For two countries can have similar percentages of information workers and have widely different standards of living. It is the work these information workers do that contributes to the level of informatization in the society. As Porat and Rubin noted in their monumental efforts to define information work, it is impossible to defined this work with any degree of certainty. Perhaps information work could better be defined by an analysis of job descriptions within a firm and within similar firms in an industry sector. However feasible this microanalysis may be, it is likely that job descriptions would vary widely among different firms, even in the highly industrialized nations, and certainly among the industrializing ones.

We elected to capture the nature of the information work force by examining the extent to which this work force contributes to the productivity of the manufacturing sector. For how productive this work force is will affect the nation's output, its Gross Domestic Product and GDP/capita, measures of its economic standard of living.

A consequence of this approach has been the recognition that the size of an information sector does not necessarily determine economic growth or development. In many of the lesser developed or industrializing nations, the information work force is broadly defined to include workers engaged by government for the provision of human services, health and welfare services. Indeed, in many low-income countries the information work force reported is a better indicator of hidden unemployment rather than the degree of informatization. Further, in countries that have attracted multinational firms engaged in the assembly of microprocessors and other computer components, workers might more appropriately be called semi-skilled factory workers, who can be easily and quickly displaced by automation and are often employed solely because of low wage rates. The information or knowledge base of such work is jealously guarded by the multinational firm, and the contribution of this work force to the GDP/capita of the host country is quite limited.

While the contribution of an information sector to economic growth is essentially confirmed, we note that this relationship is not found universally across all nations, but depends on the stage of development of the country. In nations still struggling to meet such basic needs of its populace as food, housing, employment, and political security, we find that government is the employer of last resort, even for information workers who may very well have achieved a respectable level of literacy and education.

Disparities Among Nations

Disparities among nations were very noticeable in all of the measures utilized in this work. Some of the poorest nations have recorded significant growth in the informatization parameters, as expected, for they started at very low levels. The information infrastructures in the low-income nations are inadequate, and resources both inadequate and unevenly distributed. The information infrastructures in low income nations are inadequate and unevenly distributed. The information work forces are very small and if larger, are often engaged in providing health

and welfare services or are employed in make-work tasks in order to maintain political stability. Tertiary school enrollment is generally under 5% of the appropriate age group, and while literacy is increasing, it is often less than 30% of the population. These are the nations that were left out of the Industrial Revolution. To these nations, informatization is desirable, but it also presents challenges that may very well add to rather than solve their problems. How to turn the information revolution to their advantage and enhance economic growth is a major concern for policymakers in developing nations.

The Artifacts of the Information Society

The notion of an information society is visualized by most people as a technology, or with behavior that is driven by technology. Mention "information society" to the computer enthusiasts and immediately the computer comes to their minds. Mention "information society" to the communications enthusiasts, and telecommunications comes to mind. Mention the phrase to the proverbial man and woman in the street, and you are likely to be met with a surprised raise of their eyebrows, and after some thought they are likely to suggest that they do, indeed, read the newspapers fairly regularly, and a magazine or book now and then, and ask for "information" by telephone.

Since the concept of the information society was introduced in the early 1960s, social scientists have speculated widely and often quite publicly in the popular press about what technology will offer society. Computers and their capacity to store enormous amounts of information, telecommunications with the ability to access this information from anyplace, will somehow create a society that is more knowledge-centered and efficient. Routine manual labor will be replaced by cerebral information labor and, as Masuda noted, spiritual development will flourish. Some thoughtful people also saw an expanding gap between those that have access to information, the information haves, and those that do not have access to information, the have-nots.

When those who are expected to be in the forefront of awareness of the information society were questioned as to how they envisioned this new world, they responded with examples of what they perceived to be their most desired activities made possible by the emergence of the information society: working at home, push-button voting as a means to enhance democracy, increased automation to ease the need for routine work, learning via computers and computer networks, tele-shopping and other such behavioral artifacts. However, many of the randomly selected respondents said that education and training were important keys to success in this new world (Wang, 1989).

The Production of Information and Economic Growth

A conceit has been perpetuated by communications and information enthusiasts as well as futurists, creating the image of an economy that can achieve high living standards and economic growth from the pro-duction of information. This arises from the confusion about informa-tion as a primary input to an economy, or as a secondary input to the economy. In no country, not in the United States or Japan, the two leading information economies in the world, does information provide the major source of national income. In nations where information is said to be its primary source of income, one generally finds relatively low income levels and often low-value jobs. After all, information work includes data input work, which requires a minimum level of "informa-tion" skill, and telemarketing, in which the use of technology is often limited to the plain old telephone. This is not to say that a strong export-oriented film and video industry, such as that in the United States, cannot add to the GNP; but only relatively few jobs in these industries can be seen as high-value information work, which is deemed to be the hallmark of an information society. And we can always point to Singapore, the entrepot nation-state that has achieved a high standard of living from the processing and communicating of information.

An information society is one in which society is aware of the importance of information in every aspect of its work, an attitude of mind that makes for the efficient, productive, broad utilization of information in every aspect of life. Work at home can range from simply loading data into a remote computer to selling real estate with or without a computer. The former task is repetitive and routine and is likely to be low-paying, while the latter can be varied and exciting and, depending upon the knowledge and skill of the salesperson, highly rewarding. The creation of knowledge is readily recognized as important to living in any society, whether it be an industrialized one or an agricultural one; the poor farmer in India, the Bedouin in the deserts of Arabia, and the nomadic hunter in Africa are as dependent on information as is the scholar in the libraries of Oxford, Cambridge, or Harvard. All are seeking knowledge with which to improve their lot; the farmer to improve his yield, the Bedouin to guarantee the safe arrival of his caravan, the nomadic hunter to feed his family, and the scholar to find truth. The skill with which they search for and use information determines their success. And the intensity of their search is driven by how important the information is to their lives.

In everyday life today, valuable things are not necessarily badly needed unless the benefits of possession are clearly evident. The rewards information can bring are often delayed, unlike products we can hold and touch. Even the joys of reading a book can be delayed. There are, of course, exceptions. Timely information is the prerequisite for success in trading in the stock, commodity, and money markets. In the main, however, how important information is, and with that how effectively it is sought and used, are highly dependent on the work people do and their awareness of how information can help them. And one cannot overlook the importance of tradition. In a study of videotex users in Taiwan, farmers tended to disregard information that would have assisted them in selling their products at higher prices. When asked why would they choose to depend on middlemen who could and indeed did exploit them, the farmers said they felt that there was nothing wrong and they had been operating in this manner for ages (Wang, Hsu, & Kuang, 1990).

In contrast, New Zealand farmers, faced with the loss of the United Kingdom market for lamb and dairy products when the United Kingdom joined the Common Market, were very quick to transfer the research information presented to them by the Ministry of Agriculture and Fisheries, which resulted in a number of new products that soon captured equivalent markets elsewhere in Europe as well as in the United Kingdom (Dordick, 1987).

In general information services, such as those provided by videotex and other on-line services, are used by higher-educated and upper-income users engaged in business, industry, government, and academia, which reflects either that these are the traditional early adopters of innovations or that they understand the value of information (Arnal & Jouet, 1989; Chung, Wang, & Shen, 1989; Hsia & Schweitzer, 1990; Prozes, 1990; Wang, Hsu, & Kuang, 1990).

This, however, says little about how intense and efficient their search for and use of information is. For example, it has been reported that Chinese scientists and researchers spend less than 15%, on average, of their research time conducting information work, about 50% less than scientists in the United States. Further, nearly half of the research conducted at manufacturing enterprises was completed without consulting any information sources other than those obtained from previous operations (Liang, 1981a, 1981b). It is conceivable that tradition in manufacturing is adequate for an economy essentially isolated from competition. But in a world economy in which labor and capital know no national boundaries, innovation is necessary in order for a firm or a nation to hold onto its competitive position in the global economy. For the high-income nations, the challenge is to maintain and increase their living standards through high-value labor, performing high-value tasks. To do so requires the productive use of information, and to achieve that requires an awareness of the value of information to the task. It is not enough to be computer-literate or computer-efficient, rather one must be information-productive.

Information Productivity

Banks provide automated teller machines, eliminating the teller in the cage for routine transactions. Banks have provided the teller with on-line access to bank databases. Banks have significantly adopted information technology, computers, and telecommunications, and have expanded their market reach. But bankers admit that while they have reduced staff and increased profits by charging for services that in the past were offered free, their sales per employee have not increased.

Department stores have linked their intelligent and automatic cash registers to inventory, shipping, and accounting, thereby increasing control over their cash flow as well as reducing staff. But store executives complain that their salespersons have forgotten how to sell. Banks and retail establishments have greatly increased the number of transactions an employee can perform in a day, but have not increased the sales made by their employees per day. Computer processing and rapid access to data are responsible for these gains. Yet despite this technology and this access to information available to employees, they do not use this information to make the sale when the customer is "in the palm of their hand." They have achieved transaction productivity but have not yet achieved information productivity. Skill in the use of computers and other information technologies does not necessarily lead to high-value information work. Indeed, data input work is often exported by high-wage countries to low-wage countries.

Learning via computers and computer networks, and the presentation of information by means of multimedia systems, are now perceived as effective uses of information technology in education. Students can access an encyclopedia via a computer terminal; pictures and text appear on the screen. Information-seeking is made easy and attractive for the student; no longer must he or she pore through index cards and wander the library stacks. A few key words limit the search, and also the knowledge obtained. To be information-productive requires the ability to decide what information is required and when and to devise search strategies that select and simplify.

There is little doubt that information technology has made an impact on our lives, and that knowledge and information are becoming increasingly important to the working of our social systems and in our daily life. But whether they have reached the level of importance predicated by the utopians is open to question. Technological determinism has always been a threat to careful consideration of future social trends. Although Bell intentionally avoided "single-minded determinism" (Bell, 1976, p. 12) in formulating his postindustrial society, the literature cannot rid itself of the flavor of "determinism." Means and ends are too often confused in our discussion of the information society:

> Competing parables of progress and prosperity or of doom and disadvantage present the two faces of neo-technological determinism whereby these new technologies are (almost) entirely good, or (almost) entirely bad. What is common to both advocates and critics alike is the belief that telecommunications-assisted commerce and trade, and computer-assisted learning, design, manufacture and leisure could transform social life. Less evident a priori is the extent to which these technologies will remain the means by which such transformations are intentionally or unintentionally affected, or will themselves become transformed into ends. (Ferguson, 1986, p. 52)

For those who study the theories of information societies in the twenty-first century, it will not be difficult to see the mistakes others have made in the past several decades. The determinists have erred when communication messages were thought to have the effect of a hypodermic needle; they erred when development communication was treated as panacea to problems in Third World nations; and we believe they are wrong today when information technologies are portrayed as the panacea for equitable world economic growth. The challenge, for social scientists and planners who seek a transformation of today's society to a more humane information society, is to further research the extremely complex interactive relations among factors we have reviewed in this initial attempt at a holistic view of the information society. Society cannot be likened to puppet shows in which social scientists, including the economists, can predict the result by pulling a few strings. The proper study of mankind is, after all, man.

Notes

1. These criteria are: (a) an information ratio of at least 0.5; (b) per capita income of more than U.S. $10,703; (c) at least half of the work force engaged in information occupations; and (d) at least half the school age population enrolled in tertiary education.

2. A statistically significant correlation means that two variables vary with a regularity that is not pure chance, nothing more. A significant correlation does not imply a causal relationship.

Appendix A

Data Over Time by Nation Groups for Telephone,
Television, Radio, Newspaper Penetration, Literacy,
and Tertiary Education

Table 1 Telephone Penetration by Nation Groups*

	All	*Low-Income*	*Middle-Income*	*High-Income*
1970	65.4	1.7	25.4	172.4
1980	119.2	3.3	45.5	270.8
1981	135.9	2.6	55.6	293.3
1982	137.9	2.8	59.1	311.0
1983	125.2	2.4	54.8	317.7
1984	134.9	2.9	56.2	332.8
1985	138.3	2.9	58.9	337.2
1986	146.7	3.5	64.6	358.7
1987	152.2	3.7	69.7	343.6
1988	—	—	—	—
1989	165.5	4.0	79.3	384.9

*Per 1,000 inhabitants

Table 2 Television Penetration by Nation Groups*

	All	Low-Income	Middle-Income	High-Income
1970	85.4	3.8	46.3	230.3
1980	127.5	6.3	81.0	313.2
1981	132.5	5.4	89.4	323.9
1982	134.6	5.4	88.7	329.5
1983	152.1	8.5	95.6	355.6
1984	—	—	—	—
1985	146.4	9.6	120.6	347.2
1986	146.6	9.7	123.6	353.5
1987	139.9	9.8	117.7	371.9
1988	—	—	—	—
1989	163.7	15.5	132.4	386.3

*Per 1,000 inhabitants

Table 3 Radio Penetration by Nation Groups*

	All	Low-Income	Middle-Income	High-Income
1970	161.5	29.2	123.5	381.8
1980	263.2	67.6	213.5	572.3
1981	262.7	69.8	214.8	585.7
1982	272.9	80.3	219.5	582.9
1983	299.0	90.3	242.1	614.9
1984	—	—	—	—
1985	312.6	112.3	273.4	616.8
1986	319.5	118.6	283.4	643.6
1987	—	—	—	—
1988	—	—	—	—
1989	335.5	123.3	297.8	671.8

*Per 1,000 inhabitants

Table 4 Newspaper Penetration by Nation Groups*

	All	Low-Income	Middle-Income	High-Income
1970	136.0	18.1	86.5	283.9
1980	148.1	12.0	83.3	373.7
1981	—	—	—	—
1982	154.2	21.4	89.1	361.5
1983	—	—	—	—
1984	139.4	13.3	97.9	317.4
1985	—	—	—	—
1986	147.7	15.5	87.8	317.2
1987	—	—	—	—
1988	148.5	17.0	96.4	315.0

*Per 1,000 inhabitants

Table 5 Rate of Literacy by Nation Groups*

	All	Low-Income	Middle-Income	High-Income
1970	73.9	30.5	71.5	72.5
1985	69.5	44.0	72.9	86.8

*In percentage

Table 6 Tertiary Education by Nation Groups*

	All	Low-Income	Middle-Income	High-Income
1970	6.7	1.0	6.6	15.6
1980	12.3	1.5	12.2	22.0
1981	13.1	2.5	13.5	24.8
1982	13.3	3.0	13.4	25.6
1983	13.6	3.0	13.2	26.3
1984	14.1	2.0	13.5	25.1
1985	14.6	1.9	14.4	26.9
1986	14.5	2.7	14.7	27.6
1987	15.7	1.5	15.1	30.4

*In percentage of school-age population

Appendix B

Table 1   Nation Groupings by GDP/Per Capita*

High-Income Nations (in GDP/per capita)			
Spain	9330	Austria	17,300
Israel	9790	France	17,820
Hong Kong	10350	United Arab Emirates	18,430
Singapore	10450	Canada	19,030
New Zealand	12070	Germany, Fed. Republic**	19,900
Australia	14360	Denmark	20,450
United Kingdom	14610	United States	20,910
Italy	15120	Sweden	21,570
Netherlands	15920	Finland	22,120
Kuwait	16150	Norway	22,290
Belgium	16220	Japan	23,810
		Switzerland	29,880

continued

Table 1   Continued

Middle-Income Nations (in per capita/GNP)

Turkey	1370	Brazil	2,540
Botswana	1600	Hungary	2,590
Jordan	1640	Uruguay	2,620
Panama	1760	Yugoslavia	2,920
Chile	1770	Gabon	2,960
Costa Rica	1780	Iran	3,200
Poland	1790	Portugal	4,250
Mauritius	1990	Korea, Republic	4,400
Mexico	2010	Oman	5,220
Argentina	2160	Libya	5,310
Malaysia	2160	Greece	5,350
Algeria	2230	Saudi Arabia	6,020
Bulgaria	2320	Cyprus	6,260
Venezuela	2450	Ireland	8,710

Low-Income Nations (in per capita/GNP)

Uganda	250	Egypt	640
Zaire	260	Senegal	650
Mali	270	Yemen, Republic	650
Niger	290	Zimbabwe	650
Burkina Faso	320	Philippines	710
Rwanda	320	Cote D'Ivoire	790
India	340	Dominican Republic	790
China	350	Morocco	880
Haiti	360	Honduras	900
Kenya	360	Guatemala	910
Pakistan	370	Congo, People's Republic	940
Central African Republic	390	Syrian Arab Republic	980
Ghana	390	Cameroon	1,000
Togo	390	Peru	1,010
Zambia	390	Ecuador	1,020
Guinea	430	Namibia	1,030
Sri Lanka	430	El Salvador	1,070
Lesotho	470	Paraguay	1,030
Indonesia	500	Colombia	1,200
Mauritania	500	Thailand	1,200
Angola	610	Jamaica	1,260
Bolivia	620	Tunisia	1,260

Nations with especially low or high economic growth rates may move between categories, but generally speaking the groupings are rather stable.
*In U.S. $
**Germany was treated as two nations prior to unification.
Note: From World Bank, *World Development Report*, 1991, and U.S. Dept. of Commerce, *Statistical Abstract of the United States*, 1991, p. 840

Table 2 Gross Domestic Product Per Capita[1] (in U.S. dollars)

	1970	1975	1980	1981	1982	1983	1984	1985	1986	1987	1988
High-Income Nations											
Australia	2,947	—	9,820	11,080	11,140	11,490	11,740	10,830	11,920	11,100	12,300
Canada	3,844	—	10,130	11,400	11,320	12,310	13,280	13,680	14,120	15,160	16,960
France	2,275	—	11,730	12,190	11,680	10,500	9,760	9,540	10,720	12,790	16,960
Japan	1,887	—	9,890	10,080	10,080	10,120	10,630	11,300	12,840	15,760	21,020
New Zealand	2,235	—	7,090	7,700	7,920	7,730	7,730	7,010	7,460	7,750	10,000
Singapore	—	—	4,430	5,240	5,910	6,620	7,260	7,420	7,410	7,940	9,070
United Kingdom	2,194	—	7,920	9,110	9,660	9,200	8,570	8,460	8,870	10,420	12,810
United States	4,789	—	11,360	12,820	13,160	14,110	15,390	16,690	17,480	18,530	19,840
Middle-Income Nations											
Brazil	497	—	2,050	2,220	2,240	1,880	1,720	1,640	1,810	2,020	2,160
Costa Rica	569	—	1,730	1,460	1,430	1,020	1,190	1,300	1,480	1,610	1,690
Malaysia	393	—	1,620	1,840	1,860	1,860	1,980	2,000	—	1,810	1,940
Republic of Korea	265	—	1,520	1,700	1,910	2,010	2,100	2,150	2,370	2,690	3,600
Taiwan	389	970	2,348	2,683	2,654	2,819	3,134	3,234	3,897	5,169	6,177
Venezuela	1,099	—	3,630	4,220	4,140	3,840	3,410	3,080	2,920	3,230	3,250
Low-Income Nations											
Egypt	217	—	580	650	690	700	720	610	760	680	660
India	100	—	240	260	260	260	260	270	290	300	340
Philippines	186	—	690	790	820	760	660	580	560	590	630
Thailand	181	—	670	770	790	820	860	800	810	850	1,000
Zimbabwe	—	—	630	870	850	740	760	680	620	580	650

Table 3 Telephone Main Lines[2] (per 100 inhabitants)

	1970	1975	1980	1981	1982	1983	1984	1985	1986	1987	1988
High-Income Nations											
Australia	—	25.8	32.5	35.9	35.9	37.2	38.8	40.1	41.4	55	—
Canada	—	37.3	41.4	42.1	41.7	41.8	45.1	46.3	48.6	70	—
France	—	16.0	28.9	32.1	35.0	37.4	39.2	40.8	42.2	60	—
Germany*	—	22.1	33.4	35.3	36.9	38.3	40.3	42.0	43.2	65	—
Japan	—	30.0	33.1	34.0	35.2	36.0	36.7	37.8	37.1	38	—
New Zealand	—	33.1	35.1	36.1	36.8	37.1	37.5	38.3	39.4	40	—
Singapore	—	12.5	21.7	23.6	25.3	27.0	29.2	31.0	31.9	44	—
United Kingdom	—	24.1	31.7	33.1	34.1	34.8	35.8	37.1	38.3	40	52.4
United States	—	35.5	41.2	41.0	41.0	41.5	42.4	42.5	44.0	46	49.5
Middle-Income Nations											
Brazil	—	2.7	3.9	4.2	4.5	4.7	5.0	5.12	5.2	7.3	9.3
Costa Rica	—	5.2	7.1	7.3	7.8	7.9	8.1	8.2	8.1	13.7	—
Malaysia	—	4.9	3.0	3.6	4.3	4.8	5.6	6.1	6.4	9.1	—
Republic of Korea	—	4.2	7.3	8.9	10.6	12.3	14.1	16.1	18.4	—	—
Taiwan**	—	6.9	17.7	21.0	23.6	25.8	27.7	29.3	31.1	33.2	35.9
Venezuela	—	4.8	—	—	6.5	6.3	6.5	7.0	7.4	9.2	—
Low-Income Nations											
Egypt	—	.9	—	—	1.1	1.3	—	1.9	2.1	—	2.8
India	—	.3	.3	—	.3	.3	.4	.4	.4	—	.6
Indonesia	—	.2	.3	.3	.3	—	—	—	—	—	.5
Philippines	—	.8	.9	.9	1.0	.9	.9	.9	—	—	1.5
Thailand	—	.6	.8	.8	.9	.9	1.0	1.2	1.7	—	1.9
Zimbabwe	—	1.3	1.3	1.3	1.4	1.4	1.4	1.4	1.3	—	3.2

*West Germany; data obtained prior to unification
**In telephone sets/100 population

Table 4 Television Sets [4] (per 1,000 inhabitants)

	1970	1975	1980	1981	1982	1983	1984	1985	1986	1987
High-Income Nations										
Australia	220	324	381	380	428	429	—	446	472	483
Canada	333	413	443	489	460	481	—	516	546	577
France	353	361	369	375	—	—	394	402	432	467
Germany*	275	311	337	348	354	360	—	373	379	385
Japan	219	—	539	551	560	563	—	580	585	587
New Zealand	234	259	272	285	289	288	—	—	358	369
Singapore	132	153	165	170	172	188	—	195	213	234
United Kingdom	—	359	401	411	457	479	—	437	534	434
United States	413	560	684	631	646	790	—	798	813	811
Middle-Income Nations										
Brazil	64	—	124	122	122	127	—	184	188	191
Costa Rica	58	65	71	72	86	76	—	77	79	79
Malaysia	12	37	—	—	—	—	—	—	113	140
Republic of Korea	13	53	165	175	174	175	175	188	194	—
Taiwan	—	—	—	—	—	—	—	—	—	—
Venezuela	—	101	114	126	126	128	—	130	141	142
Low-Income Nations										
Egypt	16	17	34	40	41	44	—	82	83	83
India	—	.7	2.2	1.8	2.9	—	—	—	6.5	6.9
Indonesia	0.7	2.2	20	21	23	23	—	39	39	40
Philippines	11	18	21	22	25	26	—	28	36	36
Thailand	—	16	17	17	17	17	—	97	100	103
Zimbabwe	10	10	10	10	11	12	—	14	14	22

*West Germany; data obtained prior to unification

Table 5 Newspapers [4] (per 1,000 inhabitants)

	1970	1975	1980	1981	1982	1983	1984	1985	1986
High-Income Nations									
Australia	321	392	337	—	—	—	296	—	264
Canada	—	214	241	—	226	—	220	—	225
France	238	201	—	—	191	—	212	—	193
Germany*	325	367	408	—	408	—	350	—	344
Japan	511	545	569	—	575	—	562	—	566
New Zealand	375	—	345	—	325	—	—	—	328
Singapore	198	200	249	—	286	—	277	—	357
United Kingdom	—	429	451	—	421	—	414	—	421
United States	303	281	282	—	269	—	268	—	259
Middle-Income Nations									
Brazil	—	45	44	—	—	—	57	—	48
Costa Rica	102	88	71	—	77	—	72	—	—
Malaysia	72	85	—	—	—	—	—	—	—
Republic of Korea	138	—	—	—	—	—	323	—	—
Taiwan	—	—	—	—	—	—	—	—	—
Venezuela	—	89	176	—	—	—	186	—	—
Low-Income Nations									
Egypt	23	30	—	—	76	—	43	—	50
India	—	19	20	—	—	—	21	—	28
Indonesia	—	—	—	—	—	—	18	—	16
Philippines	—	—	—	—	—	—	—	—	—
Thailand	21	—	—	—	53	—	—	—	—
Zimbabwe	16	19	16	—	21	—	22	—	24

*West Germany; data obtained prior to unification

141

Table 6 Amount of Data Terminal Equipment on the Public Telephone and Telex Networks[2] (in thousands)

	1970	1975	1980	1981	1982	1983	1984	1985	1986	1987	1988	1989
High-Income Nations												
Australia	—	4.0	7.8	10.7	13.4	16.2	17.1	18.9	14.4	—	—	—
Canada	—	—	—	—	—	—	—	—	—	—	—	—
France	—	10.6	19.1	21.8	26.9	—	—	—	40.4	—	—	—
Germany*	—	—	—	46.4	51.3	60.9	71.2	86.5	106.0	—	—	—
Japan	—	—	—	—	—	.52	.55	.50	—	—	—	—
New Zealand	—	—	—	.75	.75	1.14	1.14	1.14	—	—	—	—
Singapore	—	.03	.07	.11	.10	.78	1.3	1.6	3.3	—	—	—
United Kingdom	—	45.8	66.6	81.5	93.3	98.6	—	—	—	—	—	—
United States	—	—	—	—	—	6.0	9.0	12.0	15.0	17.0	19.0	20.0
Middle-Income Nations												
Brazil	—	—	—	—	—	—	—	—	—	—	—	—
Costa Rica	—	—	—	—	—	1.7	—	—	—	—	—	—
Malaysia	—	—	—	—	—	—	.36	.81	1.9	—	—	—
Republic of Korea	—	—	—	—	—	—	—	4.1	—	—	—	—
Taiwan	—	—	—	—	—	—	—	—	—	—	—	—
Venezuela	—	—	—	—	—	.82	—	—	—	—	—	—
Low-Income Nations												
Egypt	—	—	—	—	—	—	—	—	—	—	—	—
India	—	—	.02	.10	—	—	—	—	—	—	—	—
Indonesia	—	—	—	—	.02	—	—	—	—	—	—	—
Philippines	—	—	—	—	.003	5.3	2.5	4.4	—	—	—	—
Thailand	—	—	—	—	—	.024	.04	.16	—	—	—	—
Zimbabwe	—	.001	.001	—	.01	.65	.73	.81	.96	—	—	—

*West Germany; data obtained prior to unification

Table 7 Information Sector[3] (percentage of total work force)

	1970	1975	1980	1981	1982	1983	1984	1985	1986	1987	1988	1989
High-Income Nations												
Australia	39.4	43.8	46.2	47.3	48.6	49.1	49.7	49.9	45.0	46.0	45.6	45.0
Canada	—	—	50.9	51.6	52.9	53.1	53.8	54.3	54.8	54.9	55.7	55.8
France	—	—	—	—	—	—	—	—	—	—	—	—
Germany*	—	44.1	45.3	—	47.0	45.0	46.9	47.3	46.7	46.9	47.5	47.0
Japan	—	40.7	43.0	43.6	44.4	—	45.6	45.3	45.7	—	—	47.5
New Zealand	—	—	35	—	37	—	40.0	—	48.6	49.6	51.2	52.0
Singapore	—	44.7	42.9	42.8	44.3	45.5	46.5	46.5	46.2	47.0	46.2	46.8
United Kingdom	—	—	—	—	—	—	—	—	—	—	—	—
United States	39.2	49.8	52.2	52.7	53.7	54.4	54.6	55.1	55.6	55.9	56.3	56.7
Middle-Income Nations												
Brazil	—	—	27.9	27.9	27.9	28.0	28.5	29.0	30.2	30.2	31.2	32
Costa Rica**	—	—	—	34.8	32.8	35.0	35.4	37.8	37.5	30.4	31.2	31.7
Malaysia	—	24.3	26.6	26.6	28.4	28.5	29.5	30.7	30.8	30.9	—	33
Republic of Korea	—	22.6	29.1	29.2	30.6	32.1	32.9	34.3	34.3	34.1	34.6	35.4
Taiwan***	—	28.3	31.8	32.7	33.1	33.4	33.7	34.2	34.3	35.1	37.2	38.5
Venezuela	—	34.2	38.0	38.4	38.8	39.3	39.0	38.6	38.7	39.2	39.6	40.6
Low-Income Nations												
Egypt	—	20.7	26.2	27.4	28.4	28.0	30.1	30.1	31.2	31.4	31.5	31.8
India	—	18.2	—	—	—	—	—	—	—	—	—	—
Indonesia	—	—	—	—	21.6	—	—	22.2	—	—	23.0	—
Philippines	—	—	21.9	22.9	22.8	22.4	23.6	23.7	23.8	24.0	23.9	24.9
Thailand	—	—	13.9	16.3	18.0	17.4	16.5	17.2	17.4	17.6	17.8	18.2
Zimbabwe	—	—	—	—	—	—	—	—	—	—	—	—

*West Germany: data obtained prior to unification
**Category 2 in ILO *Yearbook* not included
***Taiwan data obtained from the Taiwan *Yearbook*, 1989

143

Table 8 Contribution of Information Sector to GDP[5] (in $1,000/person)

	1970	1975	1980	1981	1982	1983	1984	1985	1986	1987	1988
High-Income Nations											
Australia	—	—	51.0	—	53.0	—	—	49.0	55.2	—	72.6
Canada	—	—	48.0	49.8	49.7	57.1	56.8	56.4	51.2	—	63.9
France	—	—	—	—	—	—	—	—	—	—	—
Germany*	—	—	50.0	—	52.7	—	49.2	49.6	70.8	71.2	73.4
Japan	—	—	43.7	46.3	42.4	—	47.7	50.5	73.2	85.8	96.6
New Zealand	—	—	35.0	—	—	—	—	—	36.1	—	31.2
Singapore	—	—	22.8	—	29.0	31.4	33.4	32.5	32.7	—	41.7
United Kingdom	—	—	—	—	—	—	—	—	—	—	—
United States	—	—	50.0	54.6	56.3	59.7	63.4	66.8	68.7	68.3	74.9
Middle-Income Nations											
Brazil	—	—	15.0	16.7	—	18.8	—	20.1	—	22.1	—
Costa Rica	—	—	10.0	—	10.3	—	—	12.2	—	—	15.7
Malaysia	—	—	18.5	18.4	—	20.6	22.6	18.0	20.0	23.9	24.0
Republic of Korea	—	—	14.6	16.1	15.6	16.5	17.6	16.8	22.3	—	29.4
Taiwan	—	—	—	—	—	—	—	—	—	—	—
Venezuela	—	—	37.2	—	36.7	—	—	25.2	—	26.2	27.3
Low-Income Nations											
Egypt	—	—	8.8	8.5	9.2	—	8.1	—	8.2	—	8.5
India	—	—	—	—	—	—	—	—	—	—	—
Indonesia	—	—	6.3	—	7.2	—	—	6.2	—	6.4	6.8
Philippines	—	—	9.5	9.5	9.4	8.0	7.5	6.8	6.3	6.9	7.6
Thailand	—	—	9.8	10.8	9.4	—	—	9.8	9.5	10.2	10.8
Zimbabwe	—	—	—	—	—	—	—	—	—	—	—

*West Germany; data obtained prior to unification

Table 9 Contribution of Information Sector to Manufacturing Sector Productivity[6]

	1970	1975	1980	1981	1982	1983	1984	1985	1986	1987	1988
High-Income Nations											
Australia	—	—	—	—	2.46	2.52	2.59	2.56	2.61	—	2.85
Canada	—	—	2.78	2.81	2.74	2.85	2.66	2.82	2.88	—	3.10
France	—	—	—	—	—	—	—	—	—	—	—
Germany*	—	—	—	—	3.21	—	3.17	3.04	3.42	—	—
Japan	—	—	3.10	3.12	2.99	2.94	3.03	3.10	3.44	3.55	3.65
New Zealand	—	—	—	—	—	—	—	—	2.64	—	—
Singapore	—	—	2.26	2.52	2.46	2.52	2.59	2.56	2.61	—	2.85
United Kingdom	—	—	—	—	—	—	—	—	—	—	—
United States	—	—	2.77	2.84	2.84	2.88	2.91	2.92	2.93	2.93	3.03
Middle-Income Nations											
Brazil	—	—	—	2.89	—	3.23	—	—	—	—	—
Costa Rica	—	—	—	—	—	1.02	1.18	1.22	1.32	—	—
Malaysia	—	—	3.03	2.91	—	2.80	2.76	2.76	—	—	2.25
Republic of Korea	—	—	2.79	2.78	2.70	2.68	2.69	2.63	2.70	2.88	3.20
Taiwan	—	—	—	—	—	—	—	—	—	2.88	—
Venezuela	—	—	3.44	3.35	3.24	—	2.89	—	2.49	—	2.71
Low-Income Nations											
Egypt	—	—	2.23	2.04	1.98	—	1.90	—	—	—	—
India	—	—	—	—	—	—	—	—	—	—	—
Indonesia	—	—	—	—	2.23	—	—	1.96	—	—	—
Philippines	—	—	2.77	2.86	2.81	2.47	2.04	1.84	1.68	1.83	1.92
Thailand	—	—	—	2.90	2.50	—	—	2.80	2.90	—	—
Zimbabwe	—	—	—	—	—	—	—	—	—	—	—

*West Germany; data obtained prior to unification

Table 10 Rate of Literacy (in percentage)

	1970	1975	1980	1981	1982	1983	1984	1985	1986	1987	1988	1989
High-Income Nations												
Australia	—	—	—	—	—	—	—	99.0	—	—	—	—
Canada	—	95.6	—	—	—	—	—	99.0	—	—	—	—
France	—	—	98.8	—	—	—	—	—	—	99.2	—	—
Germany*	—	—	—	—	—	99.1	—	99.0	—	—	—	—
Japan	—	—	—	—	—	—	—	99.0	—	—	—	—
New Zealand	—	—	—	—	—	—	—	99.0	—	—	—	—
Singapore	68.9	—	82.9	—	—	—	—	86.1	—	—	—	—
United Kingdom	—	—	—	—	—	—	99.0	99.0	99.1	—	—	—
United States	—	—	—	—	—	—	—	99.2	99.1	99.2	99.2	99.1
Middle-Income Nations												
Brazil	66.2	76.8	74.5	—	—	—	—	77.7	—	—	—	—
Costa Rica	88.4	—	—	—	—	92.6	93.6	—	—	—	—	—
Malaysia	58.0	—	69.6	—	—	—	—	73.4	—	—	—	—
Republic of Korea	87.6	—	—	92.7	—	—	—	—	—	—	—	—
Taiwan	79.4	84.2	82.7	88.4	88.9	89.4	89.9	90.4	90.8	91.2	91.7	—
Venezuela	76.5	84.6	—	—	—	—	—	86.9	—	—	—	—
Low-Income Nations												
Egypt	—	38.2	—	—	—	—	—	44.5	50.7	—	—	—
India	34.1	—	—	41.0	—	—	—	43.5	—	—	—	—
Indonesia	56.6	—	67.3	—	—	—	—	64.1	—	—	—	—
Philippines	82.6	—	83.9	—	—	—	—	85.7	—	—	—	—
Thailand	78.6	81.5	88.0	—	—	—	—	91.0	—	—	—	—
Zimbabwe	—	—	—	—	77.8	—	—	74.0	—	—	—	—

*West Germany; data obtained prior to unification

146

Table 11 Number of School-Age Population Attending Tertiary Schools (per 1,000)

	1970	1975	1980	1981	1982	1983	1984	1985	1986	1987	1988	1989
High-Income Nations												
Australia	16.6	24.0	25.4	26.0	26.0	26.0	27.0	27.6	28.8	26.0	—	—
Canada	34.6	39.3	42.1	37.0	39.0	42.0	51.6	55.5	54.8	58.2	—	—
France	—	24.5	25.5	26.0	27.0	28.0	29.2	29.8	30.0	30.9	—	—
Germany*	—	24.6	26.2	28.0	30.0	30.0	29.4	29.9	30.1	—	—	—
Japan	17.0	24.6	30.5	30.0	30.0	30.0	29.8	28.7	28.9	28.3	—	—
New Zealand	18.4	25.7	28.6	26.0	26.0	28.0	—	29.5	33.0	32.0	—	—
Singapore	6.8	9.0	7.9	8.6	10.3	11.8	—	—	—	—	—	—
United Kingdom	14.0	18.8	20.1	19.0	22.2	21.7	21.8	22.3	—	—	—	—
United States	49.4	57.3	56.0	58.0	57.1	56.7	56.7	59.6	—	—	—	—
Middle-Income Nations												
Brazil	5.26	10.7	11.9	12.0	12.0	11.0	—	—	10.5	10.9	—	—
Costa Rica	10.3	17.7	23.3	26.0	27.0	26.0	21.9	22.7	23.3	24.8	—	—
Malaysia	—	—	4.3	5.0	4.0	5.1	6.0	6.9	6.8	—	—	—
Republic of Korea	9.1	10.3	17.0	18.0	24.0	24.0	—	35.5	35.3	36.7	36.5	36.7
Taiwan	—	—	—	—	—	—	—	—	—	—	—	—
Venezuela	11.7	16.4	20.4	20.0	22.0	23.4	25.6	24.9	24.9	25.6	—	—
Low-Income Nations												
Egypt	7.9	13.5	17.6	15.0	15.0	16.0	20.0	20.2	20.4	20.0	—	—
India	4.4	8.6	—	9.0	8.9	8.9	—	—	—	—	—	—
Indonesia	2.7	2.4	3.8	3.0	4.0	5.6	6.3	—	7.0	—	—	—
Philippines	19.9	18.4	27.7	26.0	27.0	26.0	34.1	38.0	38.0	—	—	—
Thailand	2.0	3.5	13.1	20.0	22.0	—	19.6	20.0	—	—	—	—
Zimbabwe	—	1.6	1.3	—	1.0	3.0	2.8	3.2	3.7	—	—	—

*West Germany; data obtained prior to unification

147

Notes

1. GDP/capita data from the *World Development Report*, World Bank, 1989, NY: United Nations; and Baring Securities/Jardine/IFS.

2. Telephone main lines and data terminal equipment from International Telecommunications Union, *Yearbook of Common Carrier Telecommunications Statistics* (15th edition), 1988.

3. Information sector data was derived from the International Labour Office (ILO) *Yearbook of Labour Statistics*, various years. Information labor force (Li) calculated from the first four labor categories in the yearbook: Category 1: Professional, technical, and related occupations; Category 2: Administrative, technical, and related workers; Category 3: Clerical and related workers; Category 4: Sales workers. (When compared to the disaggregated method of identifying information workers, as used by Porat, this aggregated approach results in an error of no more than ±4%. For further details see Appendix C. Information Sector as a percentage of total labor force (L) is determined by the ratio L/Li.)

4. Television/1,000 population, Newspaper circulation/1,000 inhabitants, rate of literacy in percent, students attending tertiary schools/1,000 obtained from: United Nations, *Demographic Yearbook*, various years; *Statistical Yearbook*, UNESCO, various years; Showers, *World Facts and Figures*, 1989; The Economic Books, Ltd., 1990.

5. Contribution of information sector to GDP from *World Development Report*, World Bank, various years (noted above). ILO sources noted above. Calculated as follows: Q/Li where Q is the GDP and Li is the information labor force, as above.

6. Contribution of information sector to manufacturing sector productivity: sources same as for Note 5. Calculated as follows: log(Qp/Lp)/Li/L where Qp is the manufacturing work force, Lp is the labor force in production, Li and L defined as above.

References

Alker, H. (1966). Causal inference and political analysis. In J. Beard (Ed.), *Mathematical applications in political science II*. Dallas: Southern Methodist University Press.

Arnal, N., & Jouet, J. (1989). Teletel: A Snap Shot of Residential Use. *Technologies of Information and Society, 2*(1), 105-124.

Bagdikian, B. (1983). *The media monopoly*. Boston: Beacon.

Bailey, M. F., & Gordon, R. J. (1980). The productivity slowdown: Measurement issues and the explosion of computer power. In *Brookings paper on economic activity, No. 2* (pp. 347-420). Washington, DC: Brookings Institute.

Barnes, J., & Lamberton, D. (1976). The growth of the Australian information society. In M. Jussawalla & D. M. Lamberton (Eds.), *Communication economics and development* (pp. 128-140). New York: Pergamon.

Bell, D. (1973). *The coming of post industrial society: A venture in social forecasting*. New York: Basic Books.

Bell, D. (1976). The social framework of the information society. In M. Dertouzas & J. Moses (Eds.), *The computer age: A twenty-year view* (pp. 163-211). Cambridge: MIT Press.

Chaikin, S., & Mathews, W. L. (1988). Will there be teachers in the classroom in the future? . . . But we don't think about that. In R. O. McClintock (Ed.), *Computing and education* (pp. 80-90). New York: Columbia University Press.

Chung, W-W., Wang, G., & Shen, V. (1989). *A study of information and cultural change in Taiwan*. Taipei: National Cheng-Chi University. Unpublished research report.

149

Compain, B. M. (1988). Information technology and cultural change: Toward anew literacy. In B. M. Compain (Ed.), *Issues in new information technology* (pp. 145-156). Norwood, NJ: Ablex.

Dahrendorf, R. (1975). *The new liberty*. London: Routledge & Kegan Paul.

David, P. A. (1989). *Computer and dynamo: The modern productivity paradox in a not-too-distant mirror* (CEPR Pub. No. 172). Palo Alto, CA: Stanford University.

Di Martino, V., & Wirth, L. (1990). Telework: A new way of working and living. *International Labour Review, 129*(5), 529-554.

Dordick, H. S. (1987). *Information technology and economic growth in New Zealand*. Wellington: Victoria University Press.

Dordick, H. S. (1989). The social uses of the telephone. In A. Zerdick & U. Lang (Eds.), *Soziologie des telefons* (pp. 221-238). Berlin: Freie Universitat.

Dordick, H. S. (1991). Toward a universal definition of universal services. *Universal telephone service: Ready for the 21st century* (pp. 109-139). Annual Review of the Institute for Information Studies, Queenstown, MD.

Dordick, H. S., Bradley, H. G., & Nanus, B. (1981). *The emerging network marketplace*. Norwood, NJ: Ablex.

Dordick, H. S., & Dordick, G. A. (1989). *Computers, computer networks and white collar productivity*. Paper presented at the Annual Convention of the International Communications Association, San Francisco.

Dordick, H. S., & Fife, M. D. (1991, April). Universal service in post-divestiture United States. *Telecommunications Policy, 5*(2), 119-128.

Dordick, H. S., & LaRose, R. (1992). *The telephone in daily life: A study of personal telephone use*. Philadelphia: Temple University Press.

Economic Books, Ltd. (1990). *The Economist book of vital world statistics*. UK: Times Books.

Elkington, J., & Shopley, J. (1985). *The shrinking planet: U.S. information technology and sustainable development* (Paper 3). New York: World Resources Institute.

Ellul, J. (1964). *The technological society*. New York: Vintage.

Ferguson, M. (1986). *New communication technologies and the public interest*. London: Sage.

Filep, R. (1991, October). Launch vehicles and spacecraft futures. *Satellite Communications*, 14-18.

Fischer, C. S. (1992). *America calling: A social history of the telephone to 1940*. Berkeley: University of California Press.

Fox, B. (1983, July/Sept). Videocassettes: Past, present, and future, *Intermedia, 11* (4-5).

Gershuny, J. (1978). *After Industrial Society, the emerging self-service economy*. Atlantic Highlands, NJ: Humanities Press.

Hamelink, C. (1983). *Cultural autonomy and global communications*. New York: Longman.

Hardy, A. (1980, January). *The role of the telephone in economic development*. Stanford, CA: Institute for Communication Research, Stanford University.

Hawkridge, D. J., Jawarski, S., & McMahon, H. (1990). *Computers in third world schools: Examples, experience, and issues*. London: Macmillan.

Hsia, H. J., & Schweitzer, J. C. (1990). *Education as a determinant of medical information-seeking behavior among Mexican-Americans*. Paper presented at the International Communications Association Conference, Dublin, Ireland.

Huws, U., Kort, W. B., & Robinson, S. (1990). Telework: Practical experiences and future prospects. In R. E. Kraut (Ed.), *Technology and the transformation of white collar work* (pp. 135-152). Hillsdale, NJ: Lawrence Erlbaum.

IFIP working group. (1988). Volume 29. Amsterdam: North-Holland.

Ito, Y. (1981). The "johoka shakai" approach to the study of communication in Japan. In G. C. Wilhoit & H. de Bock (Eds.), *Mass communication review yearbook* (pp. 671-698). Beverly Hills, CA: Sage.

Ito, Y. (1989, May). *Major issues in information society studies.* Paper presented at the Conference on Asia's Experience in Information, Taipei, Taiwan.

Ito, Y., & Ogawa, K. (1984, March). Recent trends in johoka shakai and johoka shakai policy studies. *Keio Communication Review, 5,* 22.

Japanese Information Processing Development Center (JIPDEC). (1988). *Information white paper.* Tokyo: Author.

Jayaweera, N., & Amnugama, S. (1987). *Rethinking development.* Singapore: The Asian Mass Communications and Information Center (AMIC).

Johnstone, A., & Sasson, A. (Eds.). (1986). *New technologies and development.* Paris: UNESCO.

Jonschur, C. (1983). Information resources and economic productivity. *Information Economics and Policy, 1,* 13-35.

Juliussen, E., & Juliussen, K. (1989). *The computer industry almanac.* Incline Village, NV: Brady.

Jussawalla, M. (1986). The information economy and its importance for development of Pacific region countries. In *Information, telecommunications and development* (pp. 655-86). Geneva: International Telecommunications Union.

Jussawalla, M., & Lamberton, D. M. (1982). *Communication economics and development.* New York: Pergamon.

Jussawalla, M., Lamberton, D. M., & Karunaratne, N. D. (1988). *The cost of thinking: Information economies of ten Pacific countries.* Norwood, NJ: Ablex.

Katz, R. L. (1986, September). Explaining information sector growth in developing countries. *Telecommunications Policy, 10,* 209-228.

Katz, R. L. (1988). *The information society: An international perspective.* New York: Praeger.

Kelley, J. (1991, June 15). Information technology sales soars to $256B. *Datamation,* pp. 10-18.

Klee, H. D. (1991, March/April). The video invasion of Africa. *InterMedia, 19*(2), 27-33.

Kraut, R. E. (1989, Summer). Telecommuting: The trade-offs of home work. *Journal of Communication, 39*(3), 19-47.

Kulik, J. A. (1986). Evaluating the effects of teaching with computers. In P. F. Campbell & G. G. Fein (Eds.), *Young children and microcomputers* (pp. 159-170). Englewood Cliffs, NJ: Prentice-Hall.

Kumar, K. (1978). *Prophecy and progress.* Harmondsworth, UK: Penguin.

Kuo, E.C.Y. (1989, February). *Trends of information in Singapore.* Symposium on Information Technology and Singapore Society: Trends, Policies and Applications, National University of Singapore.

Kusnetz, S. (1957, July). Quantitative aspects of the economic growth of nations II: Industrial distribution of national product and labour force. *Economic Development and Cultural Change,* pp. 27-39.

Kusnetz, S. (1966). *Modern economic growth: Rate structure and spread.* New Haven: Yale University Press.

Lange, S., & Rempp, R. (1977). *Qualitative aspects of the information sectors.* Karlsruhe, Germany: Karlsruhe Institut für Systemtechnil und Innovationsforschung.

Lerner, D. (1958). *The passing of traditional society.* Glencoe, IL: Free Press.

Lerner, D., & Schramm, W. (Eds.). (1976). *The past ten years and the next.* Honolulu: University of Hawaii Press.

Liang, Q-W. (1981a). An assessment of all sorts of information sources. *Qingbao Kexue [Information Science], 6,* 30-40.

Liang, Q-W. (1981b). A survey and analysis of the time budget of the Chinese scientific and technological information. *Qingbao Kexue [Information Science], 2,* 36-42.

Lyon, D. (1988). The role of the information society conception in IT policy: Some international comparisons and a critique. In R. Plant, F. Gregory, & A. Brier (Eds.), *Information technology: The policy issues* (pp. 21-42). London: Manchester University Press.

Machlup, F. (1972). *The production and distribution of knowledge in the United States.* Princeton, NJ: Princeton University Press.

Martinez, M. E., & Mead, N. E. (1988). *Computer competence: The first national assessment.* Princeton, NJ: Educational Testing Service.

Masuda, Y. (1981). *The information society as post industrial society.* Washington, DC: The World Future Society.

Morgan, M., & Sayer, A. (1988). *Microcircuits of capital.* Boulder, CO: Westview.

Newman, R., & Newman, J. (1985). Information work, or the new divorce? *British Journal of Sociology, 36*(4), 497-514.

New York Times, The. (1987, June 29). Section D, p. 6.

Nora, S., & Minc, A. (1980). *The computerization of society: A report to the president of France.* Cambridge, MA: MIT Press.

NTIA (1988, October). *NTIA TELECOM 2000; Charting the Course for a New Century.* NTIA Special Publication 88-21. Washington, DC: National Telecommunications and Information Administration, Department of Commerce.

OECD. (1981). *Information activities, electronics and telecommunication technologies.* Paris: Author.

OECD: CSTP. (1989). *Programme,* p. 1.

Ogan, C. (1989). The worldwide culture and economic impact of video. In M. Levy (Ed.), *The VCR age* (pp. 230-252). Newbury Park, CA: Sage.

Oniki, H., & Kuriyama, T. (1989, May 9-11). *New information technology and the growth of the Japanese economy.* Paper presented at the International Conference on Asia's Experience in Informatization, Taipei, Taiwan, ROC.

Panko, R. O. (1990). *Is office productivity stagnant?* (Working paper 90-008). Honolulu: Pacific Research Institute for Information Systems and Management.

Parkinson, C. N. (1980). *The Law.* Boston: Houghton-Mifflin.

Pennar, K. (1988, June). The productivity paradox. *Business Week,* pp. 100-102.

Pool, I. de S., Inose, H., Takasaki, N., & Hurwitz, R. (1984). *Communications flows: A census in the United States and Japan.* Tokyo: University of Tokyo Press.

Porat, M., & Rubin, M. (1977). *The information economy: Development and measurement.* Washington, DC: Government Printing Office.

Prozes, A. (1990, Summer). The electronic information age. *Business Quarterly,* pp. 80-84.

Research Institute of Telecommunications & Economics (RITE). (1968). Introduction to Information and Communication in the Post-Industrial Society. Tokyo, Japan: Author.

Research Institute of Telecommunications & Economics (RITE). (1970). Role of Telecommunications in the Post-Industrial Society. Tokyo, Japan: Author.

Roach, S. (1983, September 22). America's technological dilemma: A profile of the information economy. In *Special economic study.* New York: Morgan Stanley.

Roach, S. (1988). Technology and the service sector: America's hidden competitive challenge. In B. R. Guile & J. Quinn (Eds.), *Technology in services: Policy for growth, trade, and employment* (pp. 118-138). Washington, DC: National Academy Press.

Rostow, W. W. (1961). *The stages of economic growth: A non-communist manifesto.* Cambridge, UK: Cambridge University Press.

Rubin, M. R., & Huber, M. T. (1986). *The knowledge industry in the United States, 1960-1980.* Princeton, NJ: Princeton University Press.

Schor, J. B. (1992). *The overworked American: The unexpected decline of leisure.* New York: Basic Books.

Schramm, W. (1964). *Mass media and national development.* Palo Alto, CA: Stanford University Press.

Schumacher, E. F. (1975). *Small is beautiful: As if people mattered.* New York: Harper Colophon.

Senghas, D. (1983). Disassociation and autocentric development. *Economics, 18,* 22.

Servan-Schreiber, J-J. (1979). *The American challenge.* New York: Simon & Schuster.

Shannon, C. & Weaver, W. (1949).*The mathematical theory of communications.* Champaign-Urbana: University of Illinois Press.

Shiba, S. (1986). Information society and education: Past experiences and new trends in Japan. In B. Sendov & I. Stanchov (Eds.), *Children in an information age* (pp. 11-28). Oxford: Pergamon.

Showers, V. (1989). *World facts and figures.* New York: John Wiley.

Smith, C. P., & Zimmerman, B. J. (1988, Summer). Microcomputers in schools: A promise unfulfilled? *Social Policy,* 17-20.

Stevenson, R. L. (1988). *Communication, development and the third world.* New York: Longman.

Telecommunications white paper. (1990). Tokyo: Ministry of Posts and Telecommunications.

The use of information technologies for education in science, mathematics and computers; an agenda for research (mimeo). (1984). Cambridge, MA: Education Technology Center, Harvard Graduate School of Education.

Todaro, M. P. (1989). *Economic development in the third world* (4th ed.). New York: Longman.

UNESCO. (1987). *UNESCO statistical yearbook.* Paris: Author.

UNESCO. (1988). *Compendium of statistics on illiteracy.* Paris: Author.

UNESCO. (1989). *World communication report.* Paris: Author.

United Nations. (1989). *International trade statistics yearbook.* New York: Author.

United Nations. (1990). *Industrial development report.* New York: Author.

United Nations Industrial Development Organization. (1989). *Industry and development: Global report* (1989/1990). Vienna: Author.

Uno, K. (1982). The role of communications in economic development: The Japanese experience. In M. Jussawalla & D. Lamberton (Eds.), *Communication economics and development.* New York: Pergamon.

U. S. Department of Commerce. (1991). *Statistical abstract of the United States, 1991.* Washington, DC: Economics and Statistics Administration, Bureau of the Census.

Verity, J. W. (1992, January 13). From mainframes to clones, a tricky time. *Information Week,* p. 53.

Voge, J. (1983). The political economics of complexity. *Information Economics and Policy, 1,* 97-114.

Wall, S. D. (1977). *Four sector time series of the U.K. labour force, 1841-1971.* London: Post Office Long Range Studies Division.

Wang, G. (1986). Video boom in Taiwan: Blessing or curse? *The Third Channel, 2*(1), 365-379.

Wang, G. (1989, May). *Information society in their mind: A survey of Asian and American college students.* Reported at the International Conference of Asia's Experience in Informatization, Taipei, Taiwan, ROC.

Wang, G., Hsu, C. S., & Kuang, S. (forthcoming). *Videotex's first step in Taiwan: A study of user reactions.* Research report to be published, Taipei, Taiwan.

Webster's new world dictionary of the American language (College ed.). (1966). New York: World Publishing.

Williams, R. (1983). *Towards 2000.* London: Chatto and Windus.

Windham, G. (1970). Political development and Lerner's theory: Further test of a causal model. *American Political Science Review, 64,* 810-814.

World Bank. (1990). *World development report.* Washington, DC: World Bank.

World VCR survey: One in three TV homes. (1991, November/December). *InterMedia, 19*(6), 6.

Yearbook of Common Carrier Telecommunication Statistics. (various years). Geneva, Switzerland: ITU.

Yearbook of Labour Statistics. (various years). Geneva, Switzerland: ILO.

Yoshizoe, Y. (1986). An economic interpretation of information flow census data. *Keio Communication Review, 9,* 58-82.

Author Index

155

Subject Index

About the Authors

Herbert S. Dordick is professor of communications and former chairman of the Department of Radio, Television and Film in the School of Communications and Theater at Temple University in Philadelphia. He is an electrical engineer with degrees from Swarthmore College and the Moore School of Electrical Engineering of the University of Pennsylvania.

Prior to joining the faculty of Temple University, he was a member of the faculty of the Annenberg School of Communications at the University of Southern California, engineering manager at the Radio Corporation of America, chief engineer of the Electronic Instruments Division of the Burroughs Corporation, a research and development engineer at the Leeds and Northrup Company, and a senior member of the research staff at the RAND Corporation. He served as a consultant to President Johnson's Task Force on Communications Policy. Professor Dordick was the first director of the Office of Telecommunications for the Commission Committee on Federal, State, and Local Cable Regulation. He was responsible for the development of the Master Plan for Cable Communications for Los Angeles and a frequent consultant to federal, state, and local governments and to industry on matters concerning communications policy, both domestic and international.

Professor Dordick was the founder and first president of the Information Transfer Corporation, a firm specializing in the development and marketing of education and training materials. He also served as president of Applied Communications Networks, Inc., which provides design and consulting services for the network services marketplace, including teleconferencing, electronic mail, and other modern communications-computer services, market research for electronic publishing, videotex, teletext, and common carriers and electronic funds transfer.

Professor Dordick was awarded a Fulbright Fellowship and the first Telecommunications Fellowship at the Institute of Policy Studies at Victoria University of Wellington, New Zealand, for research on information technology and economic growth.

Professor Dordick is the author, co-author, or editor of numerous books, and the author of more than 90 articles, book reviews, and chapters on communications and informations technology. His primary research interest is in the field of technology and society. He has pioneered in research on the social uses of the telephone and, in particular, on the personal telephone in daily life, and has recently completed a major three-country study on this topic.

Georgette Wang is professor in the Department of Journalism, National Chengchi University in Taipei, Taiwan. She obtained her Ph.D. degree from Southern Illinois University in 1977, and a master's degree from Cornell University. Dr. Wang has worked as a research associate and later as a visiting fellow at the East-West Center, Honolulu, Hawaii. She has also worked in the media in Taiwan and taught at the Chinese University in Hong Kong.

Dr. Wang's research interest has been focused on the social and cultural aspects of information technology applications. Her major English language publications include *Treading on Different Paths: Informatization in Asia* (forthcoming), and *Continuity and Change in Communication Systems*, both edited volumes. She has also published widely in the Chinese language.